Oct 8, 1932 – Jan 17, 2008

3/24/08
Linda Hannisdal

THE MEDIEVAL HEALTH HANDBOOK

TACUINUM SANITATIS

The Medieval Health Handbook

TACUINUM SANITATIS

LUISA COGLIATI ARANO

George Braziller   *New York*

Translated and Adapted by Oscar Ratti and Adele Westbrook from the original Italian edition: Luisa Cogliati Arano, Tacuinum Sanitatis, *Electa Editrice.*

Published in the United States in 1976
by George Braziller, Inc.

International Standard Book Number: 0–8076–1277–4
Library of Congress Catalog Card Number: 75–21725

First published in Italy by Electa Editrice, Milan
First paperback printing, April 1992
Printed in Hong Kong

Table of Contents

The Physician Speaks:

"THE TACUINUM SANITATIS is about the six things that are necessary for every man in the daily preservation of his health, about their correct uses and their effects. The first is the treatment of air, which concerns the heart. The second is the right use of foods and drinks. The third is the correct use of movement and rest. The fourth is the problem of prohibition of the body from sleep, or excessive wakefulness. The fifth is the correct use of elimination and retention of humors. The sixth is the regulating of the person by moderating joy, anger, fear, and distress. The secret of the preservation of health, in fact, will be in the proper balance of all these elements, since it is the disturbance of this balance that causes the illnesses which the glorious and most exalted God permits. Listed under these six classifications are many very useful varieties whose nature, God willing, we shall explain. We shall speak, furthermore, about the choices suitable to each person owing to his constitution and age, and shall include all these elements in the form of simple tables because the discussions of the sages and the discordances in many different books may bore the reader. Men, in fact, desire from science nothing else but the benefits, not the arguments but the definitions. Accordingly, our intention in this book is to shorten long-winded discourses and synthesize the various ideas. Our intention also, however, is not to neglect the advice of the ancients."

(Rouen, f. 1)

INTRODUCTION

The history of art can undoubtedly be qualified as a comparatively recent discipline if we define it as a surveying and interpreting of those images which provide us with a vivid testimony to the life and artistic development of the past as well as the present. Nevertheless, it is still surprising to note that a particular group of illuminated manuscripts of great importance has gone largely unnoticed and unremarked for centuries, even by those whose sphere of interest has been the study of the figurative arts. But such, in fact, has been the amazing fate of those manuscripts we are about to examine.

The first substantial clue to their existence came in 1895, when Julius von Schlosser mentioned a noteworthy illuminated manuscript in the Austrian Imperial Collection which bore the title, *Tacuinum Sanitatis In Medicina*. In commenting upon Schlosser's significant contribution to knowledge about this work Leopold Delisle indicated, in 1896, that there was a similar manuscript in the National Library in Paris. Then, in 1905, Professor Fogolari revealed that a third, related codex was contained in the collection of the Casanatense Library in Rome. A comparison of these three manuscripts reveals a number of obvious and exciting similarities. Moreover, we can now add two more manuscripts to this grouping, one of which is presently in Liège, while the other is in Rouen.

The *Tacuinum* in the University Library of Liège is mentioned in the catalogue of an exhibition of Western illuminated manuscripts held in Vienna in 1952, and again, by Renata Cipriani, in the catalogue of the 1958 exhibition in Milan of *Lombard Art from the Visconti to the Sforza* (where the manuscript, however, was not actually exhibited). The 1875 catalogue of the University Library of Liège had attributed this *Tacuinum* to the fifteenth century and qualified it as a *manuscrit curieux*. Undoubtedly it does pose a number of problems, as we shall see. I actually found it listed as early as 1892 in the Spanish Bulletin of the Academy of History, as a Cordovan manuscript. We shall delve later into the reasons behind this Cordovan qualification, since they are linked to the Arabian physician whose texts were the matrix for the development of the *Tacuina*.

The codex in the Municipal Library of Rouen (exhibited in 1958 in Milan) had already been mentioned as early as 1839, and had been registered in the 1888 general catalogue of all manuscripts contained in the public libraries of France. In an article published in 1950 Wickersheimer linked it to the other *Tacuina*.

Another illuminated manuscript which displayed certain affinities to those already mentioned above had been catalogued in the first half of the eighteen-hundreds as part of the collection of the National Library in Paris, and Professor Otto Pächt discussed this manuscript in an important article published in 1952-53. However, although it is obvious that the Paris manuscript is a very intriguing one, we feel it is beyond the scope of our present study and therefore will not include it among the manuscripts to be examined on the following pages.

We have also excluded two other codices, probably of Venetian origin and dating from the fourteen-hundreds, listed as MSS. 5264 and 2396 in the National Library in Vienna, in order to concentrate upon the five manuscripts which were undoubtedly conceived in the Po Valley even if they included the work of illuminators of diverse origins. In fact, all the manuscripts we will consider clearly display the manifold tendencies to be found in works done in the Po region during the course of a few decades—we may actually say within twenty years, if we exclude the last of these manuscripts, i.e., that of Rouen.

What was the reason for the success of the specific category of manuscripts represented by the *Tacuinum Sanitatis* at a particular moment in the history of the West? Why did interest in these Illuminated Medieval Health Handbooks continue unabated, even when printed editions began to replace handwritten and painted manuscripts? Furthermore, from which tradition did this genre of illuminated manuscripts spring? Upon closer inspection, we might venture to speak of illuminated manuscripts with the addition of abbreviated "commentaries." A consideration of undoubted interest is the relationship between the *Tacuinum Sanitatis* of the late 1300s and 1400s and medieval manuals on herbs. While the *Tacuina* constitute a singular category, it would seem undeniable that the fundamental source for these manuscripts is to be found in the herbalist tradition. And just as any work on medieval herbal manuscripts must contain a chapter devoted to the *Tacuinum*, so our study will draw enlightenment from the tradition of the *Herbaria*. If in a plant illustrated in the *Dioscorides Codex* of about 512 we can recognize a distant source for a similar representation in a *Tacuinum* completed at the end of the fourteenth century, we shall begin to appreciate the parallels to the written texts as well, thus gaining a more complete comprehension of the work in its totality. For example, a consideration of herbal manuals as providing either a precedent for or being contemporary with (as well, of course, as successive to) the *Tacuina* reveals a productive vein of exploration. In this context, if we wish to evaluate the state of modern studies concerned with herbal manuals, a consideration of Camus's findings will be of interest. In 1886, exactly nine years before Schlosser published his views on the *Tacuinum Sanitatis* in Vienna, Camus had acknowledged only the work of Benedetto Rinio and the famous *Dioscorides*, previously mentioned, as being unique medieval treatises with illustrations of plants. Therefore, as far as critical studies of herbal manuscripts are concerned, we find ourselves in approximately the same situation as seen above in relation to the *Tacuina*.

In any case, it is their extraordinary ability to communicate directly by means of images that makes the pages in the herbal manuscripts and in the *Tacuina* particularly fascinating today, over and above the natural interest of the scholar in identifying that period which produced the *Tacuina* (i.e., the late Gothic era).

We shall soon see that Arabic medicine is at the root of the text contained in the *Tacuina*. Only a few of the many Arabian botanical and medical treatises with which we are familiar are illustrated, but modern studies have perhaps not sufficiently underlined the fact that, just as the written text in the *Tacuina* had been translated from

Arabic into Latin, so, in all probability, a similar rapport may be found in the figurative dimension. We should not exclude the possibility that the Arabic culture of Southern Spain was a determinant factor in the passage of these texts from their Arab matrix to their European interpretations. It is not possible to consider a problem of such dimensions here, but I should mention in this connection a manuscript in the Library of Alexandria, examined by Farès, and which he had placed about the middle of the fourteenth century. This manuscript contains 270 illustrations of botanicals. The Arabic text, unpublished until Farès made it known, bears the following note in French in the Introduction:

> After the folios on animals, I present plants and minerals, according to the statements of competent doctors. I rely on their opinions, favorable or unfavorable, depending upon whether the properties of the substances being considered are useful or dangerous (to the extent that verification and checking of sources was possible for me). In the preparation of this collection, the Treatise composed by the botanist Abu Muhammad 'Abd-Allah ibn Ahmad, known by the name of Ibn al Baytar, born in Malaga, was of great help to me.

The intentions expressed in these lines do not differ substantially from those which resulted in the execution of the *Tacuina*. Therefore, we may accept the hypothesis of Arabic antecedents to the medieval health handbooks we are considering. Furthermore, there is no doubt that the method of cultivating herbs still employed in Southern Spain leads us to designs that are found on the pages of the *Tacuina*. Certain sinuous rhythms evident in climbing plants still to be seen in the open courtyards of the old quarters in Seville and Cordova were obviously the source of inspiration for many similar elaborate and elegant designs in these late Gothic manuscripts. How much of the Arabic culture filtered into the Western world, notwithstanding the repressive intentions of those who had reconquered areas previously under Arab domination, remains to be clarified.

In any case, representations of herbs, flowers, and fruits predominate in the *Tacuina* illustrations. However, there are also folios devoted to natural elements, foodstuffs, winds, and seasons. Moreover, the changeable conditions of human emotions, from anger to joy, as linked to the medico-chemical theory of humors upon which herbal compounds are considered to have such a profound influence, are certainly not neglected. And all these elements are framed within settings consistent with normal living habits—thus rooms are illustrated which would be suitable to the frigid conditions of winter and those better adapted to the summer's heat. The influence of the stars, planets, and, therefore, the climate upon the places where a man's life is lived, and also the contingent usefulness of each practice, drink, or particular kind of food, is precisely depicted on every folio. The result is a representation of life in its totality, to which the commentaries correspond in their description of the rapport between man and nature. The statement which follows is found at the beginning of the Vienna manuscript.

A Manual of Health, indicating things which should be done, by illustrating the positive side of various foods, drinks and clothing, as well as their dangerous aspects and the neutralization of these dangers through the advice of the best among ancient authorities.

The Paris and Liège manuscripts, which do not have the explanatory introduction contained in both the Vienna codex and the one in the Casanatense Library (as well as in the Rouen manuscript), list instead the names of the particular men considered to be the best among noted ancient authorities. There are sixteen names in both manuscripts, fifteen of which are probably the same. Then, in the Liège manuscript, we find *Ve* for *Vegetius* as the sixteenth entry, while *Jesus* is represented by *Je* as the sixteenth authority in the Paris manuscript.

From these specifications one can immediately sense the universal character which, in medieval times, influenced the approach to all problems related to medicine and health. In a certain sense, this idea of unity is worlds apart from the conception of life which evolved during the centuries after the emergence of the doctrine of Humanism.

According to indications found in four of the manuscripts we are considering, the author of (or at least the source of inspiration for) the precepts expressed in the written texts found in the *Tacuina* is considered to have been the Arabian physician Ibn Botlân, variously known as:

Ellbochasim de baldach	(Vienna)
Albulkasem de Baldac	(Paris)
Ububchasym de Baldach	(Casanatense)
Albullasem de baldak	(Liège)

There are many famous manuscripts on the works of Ibn Botlân in the original Arabic, among which is one in the British Museum with an interlinear Latin translation (Add. 3676). There are also many manuscripts which have only the Latin translation. Of these there is a printed edition, done in Strasbourg in 1531, dedicated to Cardinal Albert of Brandenburg. It was followed by a translation into German, published in 1533.

From a clarification of the term *Tacuinum* we can obtain an understanding of how much of the Arabian physician's text has found its way into our illuminated manuscripts. The manuscripts in Arabic, those in Latin translation, as well as the printed editions of Ibn Botlân's work contain tables divided into sections indicating vegetable and animal foods, states of mind or emotions, and meteorological conditions. In these tables we find the topics which will constitute the subject matter treated in the illuminated *Tacuina*. The succinct indications in the partitions of these tables constitute the source of the commentaries appearing beneath each illustration in the illuminated manuscripts, which explain the properties of the particular herb, food, or type of clothing represented or the effects of the seasons, emotions, etc., upon the courses of a man's life. Therefore, the illuminated *Tacuina* do not represent the exact text of Ibn Botlân's writings but, in a certain sense, their synthesis.

The term *Tacuinum* is derived from the Arabic *taqwîm*. Wickersheimer, seeing the disparity of interpretations among Arabic specialists concerning this derivation, posed the problem to a specialist, Charles Jaeger, who explained the apparent contradictions in the various interpretations of the Arabic term by proposing the translation of the term *taqwîm* as *tables*. The derivation, at this point, is clear. As each partition of a table in the Arabic manuscript indicated the properties of the subjects illustrated, so on each page of the illuminated manuscripts the work presents an illustration completed by the text commentary written below. The almost square shape of the illustrations in the *Tacuina* thus provides another link to the tables found in the original Arabic works, and the indication concerning the author who was the source of the text is further verified.

Returning to the research carried out by our Arabic specialists, we can gather much information concerning the Arabian physician Ibn Botlân, and the fortunes reserved for his work in the West (due in part, perhaps, to the fact that he was baptized under the name of John). Ibn Botlân was a student of Ibn el Taijib in Baghdad and practiced medicine in Mossul, Diyarbekir, and Aleppo. In 1047 he was in Egypt, where he engaged in a lively debate with the physician Ibn Ridwân. He was in Constantinople and in Antioch, where he retired to a monastery. He died not before 1068. He had occupied himself with theological questions, in addition to having written many works on medicine and health. This provides still further verification of the medieval tendency toward a unified view of reality rather than the analytical modes which have been the foundation of Western thought for centuries within the Humanistic framework.

Exactly when the Arabic text was translated into Latin, thus becoming a part of Western culture, has not been established with any certainty. One hypothesis is that the translation was executed in the eleventh century by Gerardo of Cremona. Certainly a translation must have been available in 1266, if we are to accept the inscription in the Latin manuscript (No. 315) belonging to the Marciana Library in Venice, which reads:

Here begins the book of the *Tacuinum*, translated from Arabic into Latin at the Court of the Illustrious King Manfred, Lover of Science.

From this inscription we can see both when and where the translation was done. Manfred was King of Sicily from 1254 to 1266 and his court was in Palermo. But this, of course, does not mean the translation done for Manfred was the first. From Delisle's investigations of the archives of the National Library in Paris it is obvious that the Latin translation of the basic text was widely distributed during the fourteenth and fifteenth centuries, at any rate. The National Library owns several such manuscripts, and Wickersheimer adds several others in various collections to the original list compiled by Delisle. Here we wish to emphasize that one was part of the Visconti Library in Pavia during the fifteenth century, as quoted by Adda and discovered by Pellegrin, who indicates its current reference number in the National

Library to be Lat. 6977A. It is in this Paris Library, as is well known, that there are a considerable number of manuscripts which were once part of the splendid Visconti Library until they were transported to France at the time of the conquest of the Milanese by Louis XII. The particular manuscript mentioned above appears on the inventory lists of 1426, and there is reason to believe that it was part of the Visconti Library during the period of its greatest expansion in the second half of the fourteenth century.

It is, therefore, probable that this Latin translation of Ibn Botlân's text presented by Ferragut at the Court of Naples was the first source of the abbreviated text which appears in our five manuscripts. Without trying, at this point, to establish a relational chronology among these manuscripts, we may state that, with the exception of the Rouen manuscript which belongs to the 1400s, all the others were completed during the last twenty years of the 1300s.

Considering the state of culture at that time, it is in keeping with the Northern Italian milieu and its court life that works of this nature, i.e., which presented a summary of everything one needed to know to live well, were in great demand. It is also obvious that they could not have been difficult and abstruse but rather immediately comprehensible to their intended readers. This secular vein ran parallel to the demands from the same aristocratic patrons for pious works such as Books of Hours—both kinds of manuscripts being capable of satisfying the exigencies of the most refined tastes.

In the milieu of the Po Valley during the last twenty years of the 1300s, the courts of the Visconti and the Scala were flourishing centers of artistic realizations of every kind. It is enough to mention the workshops of the Duomo and the Certosa, established for the Milanese by Gian Galeazzo Visconti, and of that trend in Verona which, from the Scaligeri tomb of *Can-grande* (+1329) and *Mastino* II (+1351), "opens the flowering way that leads from Altichiero through the enchanting Stefano, to that most exalted arbiter of courtly taste, Pisanello" (Fiocco). A typically international character was common to the milieu of both courts, and it was not by chance that Giovanni Alcherio of Milan and Pietro Raponda of Verona were responsible for the exchange of works of art between the courts of Italy and that of Jean, Duke of Berry. It is difficult to read the spendid incunabulum of courtly culture represented by Ms. Lat. 757 in the National Library in Paris (containing an Easter table that establishes its date as 1380) without being reminded of the extensive network of rapports, not only between Italy and France, but also linking the lands along the Danube.

We mention this manuscript which, in our opinion, belonged to Bernabò Visconti and his wife, Beatrice Regina of the Scala family, because we believe that the typology which is the foundation of the *Tacuina* is, in part, linked to one of the two veins detectable in this codex. Taking into consideration the fundamental role of the repertoires during times in which visual memory could rely only upon graphic representations, we have been able to distinguish two connectable components at the base of the Paris Ms. Lat. 757 (which gives us a clue to the *scriptorium* from which the codex emerged). The most revealing component is that expressed by the French cultural imprint detectable in the work of the illuminator who presided over the "programming" of the entire manuscript. But even more fundamental is the qualitative contribution made by those plates whose painting must be attributed to illuminators formed at the school of Giovannino dei Grassi. This is the second fundamental vein running throughout the *Tacuina.*

It is now time to relinquish the old controversy about whether the Milanese or Veronese character dominated the art of illumination in the Po Valley during the last twenty years of the 1300s in various codices, in favor of a more comprehensive interpretation. It is certainly possible that the same Giovannino dei Grassi who set the date of 1370 on plate BR-2 in *The Visconti Hours* was a presence of such magnitude in the Northern Italian artistic environment that he dominated the Visconti and Scaligeri courts (both of which, as we have seen, were constantly in communication with one another, due in no small part to the family ties between them). Furthermore, the formation of Giovannino himself may lead us to the Bohemian schools, and the indirect contribution which may thus have been made by these schools to several Northern Italian manuscripts is a fascinating subject which scholars are now only beginning to consider.

If the rapport with France has already been discussed in Durrieu's studies during the early 1900s, the rapport with Bohemia has only been touched upon very lightly by Toesca and Arslan. But recently, Rasmo has attributed the decoration of the apartments of the Bishop of Trent to a Bohemian artist—a hypothesis already advanced and conditionally accepted by Magagnato in the catalogue of the 1958 exhibition in Verona. Of these apartments, the decoration of the great hall with frescoes depicting the cycle of the months is still extant. (This hall is generally referred to as the *Torre dell' Aquila*—Eagle Tower or Tower of the Eagle—since it was adapted from the earlier tower built over the Aquila gate near the *Castello del Buonconsiglio* in Trent.)

It is important for us to underline the fact that in dealing with the problem of the *Tacuina* we shall have to take into account, on the one hand, those authentically Lombardian and Veronese elements (noting that the comparison made by Fogolari in 1905 between certain Veronese frescoes presently in the Castelvecchio and the Vienna *Tacuinum* are still valid today) and, on the other hand, a more ample horizon which ranges from France to Bohemia. If, considering the present state of studies available, the following indication is confirmed only by a few comparisons, it is still a fundamental affirmation to be able to say that Giovannino dei Grassi, who has so often been acknowledged as the quintessential expression of the Lombard spirit, was in all probability of Bohemian formation. This does not, in our opinion, diminish the importance of the Lombardian contributions to European art, but instead, in a certain sense, increases their value by accentuating that element of internationality which made this region the meeting place for the most fertile encounters between North and South. It is sufficient to glance at the annals of the Duomo to verify how the local and the transalpine presences were superimposed one upon the other in almost every artistic realization. Undoubtedly, another unifying factor in the cultural milieu of the Po Valley was Giotto, who was not only an important presence in Lombardy during the first half of the 1300s (his patron in 1333 being Azzone Visconti), but also an influential figure in the Eastern region of that same valley, as demonstrated by the Scrovegni Chapel in Padua.

When in 1947 Coletti chose the subtitle *I Padani (The Artists of the Po Valley)* for the third volume of his work intended as a revision of *I Primitivi (The Primitives)*, he was correctly defining the problem of the geographical delimitation of Northern Italian culture by the Po Valley, which, notwithstanding its multiple aspects, also exhibits certain common characteristics. Altichiero's cultural preparation undoubtedly presents analogies to that of Giovanni Alcherio of Milano, and a knowledge of their frescoes is among the elements which characterized the *scriptoria* from which emerged the illuminated manuscripts of the last twenty years of the 1300s.

After the substantial revision in previous interpretations made possible by the exhibition of *Lombard Art from the Visconti to the Sforza*, Arslan had acknowledged that he was forced "to abandon the tendency to attribute to only one artist the illuminations that decorate each manuscript; and to think instead of a codex as having been produced in a *scriptorium* where, together with a master (or several masters), there were usually various collaborators at work."

The situation in the Northern Italian *scriptoria* (as I believe was true of all medieval *scriptoria*) has distant roots. It is sufficient to think of the function of certain codices that have been the prototypes for successive realizations, and of the strict rapport that one can discern between the sculpted decorations embellishing Romanesque churches and the plates in the various illuminated manuscripts. A typical way of working in collaboration was also evident in the stonecutters' workshops (think of the Como masters) and the method adopted by the medieval *scriptoria*.

We might then ask whether that unifying character displayed by European art for about half a century between the thirteen- and fourteen-hundreds was not perhaps the final impressive example of this communal approach to artistic realizations before Humanism, that great turning point, began to characterize Western culture in the centuries to follow with its emphasis upon the primacy of individual contributions.

THE "TACUINUM" OF LIEGE
—The Workshop of Giovannino dei Grassi

In order to determine the significance of the flowering of works of art such as the *Tacuinum Sanitatis* at a particular cultural moment, it seems fundamentally important to try to establish a relational chronology for the five manuscripts we are considering and to clarify the rapports among them. This method of investigation must take into consideration the rapports between these manuscripts and other contemporary works of art, while allowing us not only to isolate those elements which are the particular characteristics of each codex, but also to perceive that particular scientific component at the basis of both the written text and the illustrations which is undoubtedly present.

In this sense, the weight of the Arabic tradition to which we owe the text of the *Tacuinum* should not be underestimated, since that tradition actually constituted a determinant factor in the arrangement of the illustrations as well (see above, where various decorated Arabic manuscripts are discussed).

In this connection I should like to mention one of the interesting Arabic codices in the National Library in Paris, Ms. Arabe 4947. This manuscript contains a significant fragment of the Arabic translation of *Dioscoride's* text executed in the eleventh century, and therefore it represents one of the oldest manuscripts of *Dioscoride's* text still extant. The numerous illustrations with which it is decorated are stylistically connected to those used to decorate the Greek manuscripts of the same text. It is a demonstration of how well the Arabian culture received the Greek tradition, and it is not without significance that, at the moment when the Christian refused to occupy himself with medical problems, it was the Arab world which adopted the "scientific" tradition in order to resubmit it to the West (enriched by the Arabic contributions) at a later date. We must not forget that the Christian Middle Ages shunned any concentration upon the human body, since it was "matter," underlining the dualism between body and soul and accentuating the supremacy of the latter. Thus there was an abandonment of certain sectors of interest to infidel doctors, infidels by whom, however, even the most aristocratic personages did not refuse to be treated. In the curious situation thus created by Christian medieval culture is found the justification for the realization of a work such as the *Tacuinum,* wherein the most authentic Arabic tradition coexists in perfect harmony with the most refined Gothic and courtly configurations.

The manuscript in Liège is of particular interest to any consideration of the development of the *Tacuina*. The manuscript has never been published before, and we are grateful to the Director of the Liège University Library, Professor Hoyoux, for allowing us to reproduce so many of its plates here.

The history of criticism concerning this manuscript is a very unusual one. Eugene Dognée had already mentioned it in 1892 in the *Bulletin* of the Academy of History, published in Madrid. But this scholar, who had understood so well the focus of the manuscript itself, had been induced to list it as a Spanish manuscript in his attempt to reconstruct the personality of the author to whom he intended to link the text. On f. 1 of the manuscript, in fact, we read:

Albullasem de baldac   Albullasem de baldac
filius habdi medici   son of habdi the physician
composuit hunc librum   composed this book.

We have seen that today the Arabian physician mentioned in the various codices is generally acknowledged to have been Ibn Botlân, who was born in Baghdad and died not before 1068. Dognée, however, had referred this work to another Arabian physician, a native of Cordova, who died there in 1122. This author has been credited with various manuscripts cited by Casiri in the 1760 catalogue of the Escorial Library. Undoubtedly, the name in the Escorial manuscript seems very similar to that cited in the *Tacuina*. Casiri lists it in the index as "Khalaf ben Abbas Abulcassem, commonly called Alzahravi." Several works on medicine are attributed to this author, but none of these includes a *taqwîm*.

I cannot entirely exclude the possibility that the confusion between the two Arabian doctors, one from Baghdad (the author of the *Taqwîm es sihha,* from which the abbreviated texts in the *Tacuina* have been derived) and the other doctor from Cordova, author of various medical works, originated at the end of the 1300s as a result of early attempts to synthesize the teachings contained in the *Taqwîm*. Undoubtedly, the name of the physician from Cordova presents the possibility of greater association with those listed in the manuscripts. The question is not one of primary importance to an understanding of the *Tacuina*, but it is probably this attribution of the Liège manuscript to the Cordovan school, due to the confusion of names, which has determined its isolation up to this point.

The quality of the illustrations was noted by Dognée, who referred to the artist as "a draftsman of great talent." For us, after all the studies that have been dedicated to the Lombard artistic milieu, the referral of the illustrations to this area is greatly facilitated. But we should like to go even further and detect in those plates additional confirmation of the importance of Giovannino dei Grassi to the Northern Italian milieu. A fundamental point which must be clarified in establishing the moment when Giovannino's presence might have been determinant for the evolution of art, not only in Lombardy but in all of Northern Italy, is the acceptance or rejection of 1370 (the date which, it seems to us, is indicated quite clearly on f. BR-2 of *The Visconti Hours*). We had considered the problem resolved, but the negative opinion concerning this which has been expressed by such an authoritative scholar as Millard Meiss induces us to return to this subject again. In his Introduction to *The Visconti Hours*, published in facsimile in 1972, Professor Meiss reverts to the position held by Toesca, suggesting that Giovannino dei Grassi "began work on *The Visconti Hours* in the later eighties."

I should like to present a few considerations at this point. The codex in its entirety has belonged to the National Library in Florence only since 1970 and, notwithstanding the courtesy of the previous owners of the *Banco-Rari* portion, i.e., the descendants of that very same Gian Galeazzo Visconti for whom the manuscript had been realized, it was often not very easy, due to the valuable nature of the work, to study it closely. Therefore, Toesca must have seen but perhaps not studied it as minutely as he had been able to consider that portion of the manuscript once owned by the Landau-Finaly family, which was presented to the National Library in Florence in 1949 in accordance with the wishes of its last owner, Horace Finaly. We might add that soon after, in 1951, Toesca offered the entire reproduction of this section with an illuminating commentary. It does not appear to me that the *Banco-Rari* portion of the manuscript, formerly belonging to the Visconti family, was ever photographed in its entirety until very recently. After Toesca, it was not until the great exhibition in 1958 of *Lombard Art from the Visconti to the Sforza* that the problem was taken up again. Upon this occasion, however, it was also possible to study only the *Landau-Finaly* portion, since this alone was exhibited. Cipriani, who also saw the *Banco-Rari* portion, was the first to note, as far as I know, the date cited on f. BR-2 as "a date that, at first glance, seems 1320, but must be read as 1370 or 1380." After the Milan exhibition, Arslan concentrated his attention upon the history of Lombardian illumination. Notwithstanding his scholarly caution, we read that "the date 1370 which one believes can be read on *The Expulsion of Joachim From The Temple*, could, therefore, also be correct." Arslan, too, examined the codex when it was still owned by the Visconti family (I believe he saw it in a bank vault); otherwise he would probably not have had any doubts as to the correct reading of the date.

Now, however, Professor Meiss states that he cannot find anything similar in Lombardy at that time. This observation validates, in my estimation, the hypothesis of the Bohemian formation of Giovannino dei Grassi, who probably had just arrived in Milan in 1370. In fact, the convincing comparisons that both Arslan and Toesca make are with Bohemian manuscripts—Toesca mentioning the illuminations of the *Evangeliario* of 1368 by Giovanni da Troppau, Cod. 1182 in the National Library in Vienna; and Arslan the *Liber Viaticus* of Bishop Johannes Noviforensis in the Library of the National Museum in Prague, written and illuminated after 1360. The dating of these two codices is exceedingly indicative that the 1370 date is a valid one for the beginning of work on *The Visconti Hours*. It is also a way of verifying once more the impartiality of Toesca's judgment, since this scholar, although he had proposed a later date for *The Visconti Hours*, acknowledged its rapport with a work that would have preceded it by several years. Professor Meiss's statement that there is nothing similar offered for observation in Lombardy at about that time therefore seems quite true. For if it was Giovannino dei Grassi who introduced forms of this extraordinary novelty, it would have been impossible for them to have permeated the Lombardian milieu before 1370.

The primary activity of Giovannino, we can surmise, was that of miniaturist, even if he also reveals a perhaps uncommon attention to the architectural details that often enliven his miniatures. As he became increasingly involved with the problems inherent in the construction of the Duomo, he turned his attention toward sculptural and architectonic realizations. To prove this point, we note that in the Duomo's annals he is cited first as painter, and only later as headmaster and sculptor. It is highly probable that in many cases he provided the drawings, leaving the executions to others. In this we fully agree with Professor Meiss in considering that the well-known *Samaritan at the Well* in Aquila is probably to be linked to him only for the preparatory drawing. The acute analysis of Griseri, who identified its character as being essentially Burgundian, seems to me to be acceptable as far as the placing of the problem is concerned, but debatable in relation to the conclusion of attribution to Giovannino, exactly on the basis of an international interpretation of his art. However, whether one wishes to accept the opinion of Professor Meiss or that of Griseri, the character of Giovannino dei Grassi as its source of inspiration remains unchallenged.

I have discussed at sòme length the problem of the initial date which may be accepted in connection with *The Visconti Hours* because to that date is linked the possibility of dating with certainty, during the ten years between 1370 and 1380, the execution of the drawing book in the Town Library of Bergamo said to be by Giovannino dei Grassi. The similarities among the illuminations of animals, above all, along the borders of *The Visconti Hours*, which have been attributed to its earliest realization, and those drawn on the Bergamo plates are very striking. In comparing the leopards in f. BR-2v, the eagles and the deer in f. BR-48, the deer and the dogs in f. BR-115 (all in *The Visconti Hours*) with the analogous figures in f. 1, f. lv, f. 2, f. 2v, f. 4v, and f. 5 of the Bergamo drawing book, we feel certain not only that we are faced with the work of the same artist in both cases, but also that they were realized during a fairly close span of time.

Now, if we compare the Bergamo drawings with various folios in the Liège manuscript, we have the distinct impression that we are confronted with examples produced in the same cultural climate. In a certain sense, the rich series of drawings that are offered in the Liège manuscript reinforces the idea we have conceived of Giovannino on the basis of *The Visconti Hours,* of the Bergamo drawings, of the capitals realized from the drawings done for the Duomo in Milan, of the illuminated folios of the *Beroldo*, released from his workshop after his death.

In the Liège manuscript we also see confirmation of a way of working which must have been one of Giovannino's trademarks: that of giving basic information and direction concerning the realization of a work and then entrusting his workshop with a substantial part of its execution. Giovannino's direct intervention, hypothesized for the realization of the first folios as I shall endeavor to define precisely later on, reveals an immediate adherence to reality which translates into the adoption of a very new technique which, in these terms, cannot be compared to that detectable in any other manuscript known to me. In the Liège manuscript we are confronted with a book of drawings, rather than an illuminated manuscript, which exhibits a precise interest in drawing intended not so much as a preparatory stage for successive realizations, but rather as a definitive expression in and of itself. It is thus that we must understand the singular chromatic integration of the first folios where the naturalism of the figures is reinforced by the precise chromatic comparison with the colors lent by nature to plants, fruits, and shrubs adhered to in the various representations. The truly exceptional state of preservation of the manuscript allows us to verify fully the novelty of matching the drawings in sepia ink with the tender green of the naturalistic elements enlivened by the brilliant chromatic insertions represented by the fruits. It would seem that, in the wholeness of the pages containing written text and decoration or illustration, there was a singular capacity to integrate and reinforce the various elements.

The problem of the execution of the Liège manuscript poses questions analogous to those presented by *The Visconti Hours*. Initiated under the direction of Giovannino, who personally set his hand to the work on a number of the folios, the time of its execution must have been protracted by the contribution of various artists at diverse levels. The excellent condition of the codex allows us, even now, to reconstruct its original composition. In its initial plan the folios were probably tied in fours, and the separate gatherings must have originally been entrusted to various artists in the workshop. Substantial dissimilarities in quality often coincide with this subdivision of the codex into gatherings. I should like to put forward the hypothesis that the manuscript was begun sometime about 1380. Its execution then may have been a protracted one throughout the years that followed (a story similar to that of *The Visconti Hours* for which, in addition to the date of 1370, I have proposed another reference point by suggesting the year 1394 for f. LF-17 in the *Landau-Finaly* part of the manuscript). It is worthwhile remembering that among the *Landau-Finaly* folios there are also notable contributions by Giovannino, even if the major part of the decoration was the work of Belbello da Pavia and his helpers. With this indication of Giovannino's name and the proposed dating of the beginning of work on the Liège manuscript as being about 1380, we do not wish to attribute the totality of its execution to Giovannino's hand, but rather the idea of the work as a whole.

In the sequence of the illustrated subjects in the *Tacuina* there appears a certain logic of exposition that we shall see was always maintained in the manuscripts in Paris, Vienna, and Rome, but that will be progressively weaker in the later manuscript currently in Rouen. On the folios in the Liège manuscript are listed food and drinks; then the various moments of life, with its manifold states of mind, ranging from anger to joy, are successively studied. The environment within which a man lives his life is thus evoked, and mention is made of the conditioning derived from the changing of the seasons and also from the variety of locales where life unfolds.

The first folio shows the portrait of the author of the work sitting at a desk which supports a large, open book bearing the inscription described in the previous section. It is, in our opinion, a typical illustration of the late 1300s which recalls many other frescoes and illuminations, from Tommaso of Modena to Altichiero, to mention only a few examples. This, however, is seen from an iconographical point of view, not a stylistic one. The manner of drawing is typical of the Lombard school, meticulous in the description of particulars with an evident taste for the analytical, along the lines developed by Giovanni of Milan. On the lower portions of the page are indicated in abbreviated form the names of men of wisdom to whom are linked the teachings that will be expressed below the various illustrations appearing on the folios which follow. Dognée explains them all and gives evidence of a rare critical acumen when he states that our manuscript represents, in all probability, a summary of a larger work—but he acknowledges its completeness as having been derived from a prearranged design. Among the names listed appear, according to the proposed reading, Hippocrates, Galen, Rufus of Ephesus, one presupposes Dioscorides, perhaps Aemilius Macer, author of a treatise on the virtues of herbs, Vegetius, as well as certain other famous Arabian physicians. It is not our task here to clarify the written text, but these indications can help us to attain a better understanding of the figurative aspects of the work (which can only be considered as a whole, with such notes of explanation). And we may speculate that it must have been particularly congenial to Giovannino's inquisitive spirit to have programmed the entire decoration of this manuscript, for whose final execution he probably had the assistance of other artists in his workshop.

Folio 2, with the illustration of a fig tree up into whose branches a youngster has climbed (the child being intent upon gathering its fruits), is linked to f. 69v in the famous manuscript Lat. 6823, Manfredus de Monte Imperiali *De naturis auri argenti et herbarum*. The manuscript belonged to the Visconti Library in Pavia and it is probable that it was known to Giovannino dei Grassi. Pellegrin has already noted its Milanese characteristics insofar as calligraphy and decoration are concerned (I have proposed its date of execution as having been approximately 1360–75).

If my hypothesis concerning the date of the Liège codex is valid, the Manfredus de Monte Imperiali manuscript was, at that time, a recent acquisition of the Visconti Library, and therefore the codex must have been prominently exhibited. By associating it with Ms. 296 of the Lucca Library which contains, among others, the text of the Pseudo-Apuleius *De herbarum virtutibus*, I have had occasion to demonstrate that the Paris manuscript, in its plan as a "Manual on Herbs," can be linked to the most authentic Northern Italian tradition. The naturalistic taste of the ancient manuals on herbs thus constitutes the foundation for the most complex Gothic culture. Among these manuals on herbs must be included the Arabic examples of the genre, such as Ms. 3355 in the Town Library of Alexandria.

Returning to our consideration of the workshop of Giovannino dei Grassi, another clue appears significant. The Paris codex is in evident rapport with the *Historia Plantarum* of the Casanatense Library in Rome (Latin codex 459). Cipriani actually maintains that the latter was a derivation of the older manuscript of Manfredus de Monte Imperiali. I would not go that far, preferring rather to propose that the evident rapports may have sprung from a knowledge of common sources in the ancient manuals on herbs.

However, the manuscript in the Casanatense Library is now unanimously acknowledged to be the work of the school of Giovannino dei Grassi. Toesca, in fact, recognizes the hand of Giovannino himself in the execution of certain folios. There is, therefore, an important confluence of indications to which we shall return later when considering various illustrations.

As concerns the Liège manuscript, we should like to specify that we believe Giovannino's intervention possible from f. 1v to f. 9v, which are those drawn with a greater finesse. The remainder of the folios show the typical characteristics of his school, but the figures do not reveal the extraordinary elegance of those in the first folios, which can easily be compared to the noted figures in the Bergamo drawing book. The same fluid line apparent in the drawings, the assiduous attention to the ornamental detail in the clothing, the meticulous care taken in sketching the feminine hair-styles and, above all, that stylized manner, typically Gothic, according to which the folds of gowns or the outlines of footwear are expressed in forms of extreme linearity, indicate the presence of a hand of high quality. The representation of grapes on f. 2v evidences the artists's capacity to give life to the man-nature rapport with exceptional brilliance. Although within the sphere of late Gothic style, notes of vivid realism are perceivable in this drawing. The child gathers handfuls of grapes and the young woman kneeling admires, almost in amazement, the rich bunch of grapes just gathered. None of the figures in the other *Tacuina* will exhibit the vitality apparent on this page. In the Paris manuscript, a linearity of Gothic taste prevails in the folio devoted to grapes, translated, however, with a lesser skill owing to which the whole has a certain fixity. It is certainly a folio attributable to one of the less gifted illuminators of the Paris codex. Somewhat better executed is the similar illustration in the Vienna manuscript where, as in Paris (and as is true in the other manuscripts), the vine is sustained by trees among whose branches some birds are fluttering, while a woman (who certainly does not have the supple elegance of Giovannino's figures) gathers the grapes. The related folio in the Casanatense manuscript offers only the naturalistic elements, without the human presence, and it does have a certain style. From this was certainly derived the plate in the Rouen codex where, as always, the representations were evidently done at a later date, and the earlier forms have been translated into designs of a decadent stylishness.

The illustration of peaches shown on f. 3 in the Liège manuscript offers a refined portrait of a gentleman which can be compared with other figures of seated men that illustrated examples of Lombard culture had shown attired according to the fashion of the day. The manner of fringing the bottom part of the doublet is similar to that shown in the attire of figures on f. 5v of the Bergamo drawing book. Among the illustrations of the same subject in the other codices, the most felicitous is that in the Paris manuscript, attributed to an illuminator of certainly greater sensitivity as compared to the one responsible for the folio on grapes; the feminine figure, primarily in the measured gesture of the hand holding the stick to dislodge the peaches from the tree, expresses an elegant modulation of line belonging to a taste typically courtly. The figure represented in the folio of the Vienna codex, by comparison, is more fossilized, while the two similar figures in the Casanatense and Rouen manuscripts (evidently in rapport with one another) have removed the human element entirely from the composition.

The prunes and the pears, the sweet and sour pomegranates, as well as the quince (sweet as well as sour), apricots, blackberries, medlars, sweet and sour cherries, sweet almonds, are all pretexts seized upon by Giovannino in order to produce delightful sketches of the countryside where, in a certain sense, adherence to nature and courtly taste integrate one another with effects of the highest artistic quality.

From f. 10 (rucola or garden nasturtiums) of the Liège manuscript, architectural inserts become frequent. Thus a less rural environment is introduced, with the presence of human life in an inhabited center becoming more frequent. Fantastic castles often rise absurdly from steep mountainsides, as on f. 21v, where truffles are represented, on f. 22v (fennel), f. 26 (beans), f. 31 (millet), f. 46 (hare meat), f. 52 (crane), f. 53v (quail), f. 74 (spring water), and finally, even more unpredictably than hitherto, on f. 83v and f. 84. Particularly evocative are the representations of interiors, whether of houses or shops. On f. 27v, a woman is intent upon preparing a broth based on cereals for a sick woman; on f. 33, another woman prepares a meal based upon wheat (over the fireplace), which is then carried by a servant—evidently to the table where it will be consumed; on f. 33v, we watch the preparation of bread, as well as on f. 34v and f. 35 (where it is specified, however, that we are dealing with whole wheat bread), the weighing of the bread taking place on f. 35v. We observe the preparation of butter on f. 39, of cheese, (ricotta being one) on f. 39v, f. 40, and f. 40v. These scenes are extraordinarily effective, conveying as they do a precise representation of how people have proceeded with the preparation of traditional meals for centuries.

The typical sense of observation and attention to detail of an exquisitely Lombardian variety are imprinted on every folio of the manuscript. The illustration of the chicken coop on f. 41v is exceptionally lively, and the contrast between the humble toil of gathering eggs and the refined attire of the woman and young girl, thus occupied, evidence the perfect coexistence of a concrete sense of life with that of courtly taste, as had rarely occurred in Europe. After all, there is no visible difference of cultural climate in the manner of representation between these exquisite figures of women that decorate many folios of our manuscript and the refined cadence of images such as that of St. Catherine of Mocchirolo, very elegant in her dress decorated with ermine tassels—an image among the most evocative in all our paintings and that can still be appreciated in the delightful chapel reconstructed in the picture gallery of Brera.

Folio 42, with its illustration of ostriches, brings us back to Giovannino's previously mentioned matrices, but it reveals an undoubtedly abused manner. It is easy to compare it with f. 256v of the *Historia Plantarum* in the Casanatense Library in Rome, and with f. 2v in the Bergamo drawing book. The reference to Giovannino's entourage is once more confirmed, but the folio might also have been executed many years later. The folios devoted to the butcher shops, from f. 42v to f. 45v, subdivided according to the kinds of meat featured (among which camel meat is also portrayed, as in the other codices), are fully flavored little scenes of life where the representations of the animals always lead us back to that assiduous interest in these creatures apparent at its highest level in the work which emerged from Giovannino's workshop and that we find continuing up through the work of Pisanello—actually a principal characteristic of art in the Po Valley since the emergence of the ancient medieval Bestiaries and the sculpted ornamentations of facades and capitals in Italian Romanesque churches. Folio 46, which refers to hare meat, is represented by a hunting scene. A similar setting, even if better realized, is perceivable in the stupendous landscapes by Pisanello in the Palazzo Ducale of Mantua, observable after its restoration.

We return now to the subject of the repertoires and the affinity of the Milanese milieu with that of Verona. The problem was clearly delineated by Magagnato, as far as illumination is specifically concerned, through the study of the Choir Books of the Capitolare Library in Verona. I believe there is no error in reading in Giovannino dei Grassi, as well as in the works expressed by his entourage, one of the fundamental components of Pisanello's art. After all, mention of this has already been made by Paccagnini concerning the problem of the *ouvraige de Lombardie,* a definition that perhaps finds its most accurate verification exactly through a careful study of the manuscript folios of the times. As irreplaceable vectors of culture, intended in its fundamental sense of adherence to life, these manuscripts determined the possibility of the simultaneous presence of multiple and analogous components in different areas at a time when communication was difficult. The means for this communication among the various centers during the 1300s and 1400s were the rapports among the courts (as had been the rapports among the various monastic centers during the Middle Ages).

Occasionally one is tempted to ask whether, in substance, painting was drawn along, almost in tow, by the decoration of the manuscripts, at least until a certain date (let us say the middle of the 1400s). The statement of the great scholar, Jean Porcher, that "medieval painting is totally, or almost totally contained in the images decorating the manuscripts," never seemed truer than when we try to capture the main threads among the hundreds of "photograms" or "visual messages" which are expressed by the illuminated folios. Later on the subject will change in response to the pressure of the changes in European society, as well as that pressure exercised by the fundamental discovery of printing. The autumn of the Middle Ages, according to Huizinga's interpretation, concludes an epoch, one where understanding, although difficult, found irreplaceable stimulation in and through a knowledge of the illuminated manuscripts, defined by Porcher as:

A museum, by definition, of difficult access, because in order to visit it one must open the books and leaf through their pages one by one; a museum richer than all others too, where the scenes are in the thousands, witnesses of life in all its forms, recording ten centuries of history.

These ten centuries, from the setting sun of the Classical world to the sunset of the Middle Ages, probably constitute the fundamental moment of a civilization that we can define in various ways (even if all labels reveal themselves as substantially false). It is the world of which we can see the forerunner in Leonardo da Vinci and, furthermore, it will be the graphic immediacy of his stupendous drawings which will offer us the measure of the new dimension. His *Ginevra Benci* will represent perhaps the first portrait truly individualized through that psychological reading of the person to which the West had not been accustomed since late Roman times.

In the world of late medieval representations portrayed on the pages of the *Tacuina*, the interest in life intended collectively, even if imprinted with a refined, courtly taste, is shown with a particular liveliness on those folios dedicated to the preparation of foods. A dish typical of Lombardy, and which still appears on the tables of the Milanese today (even if the last small shops that sell the prime ingredient for this dish are vanishing from the streets of the old quarter of Milan), with the same dialectal denomination appearing in the manuscript, i.e., the *buseca*, is cooking on f. 48v. The figure of the woman, no longer young, who is stirring the meal cooking over the brazier, was certainly not traced by one of the most refined illuminators. It is sufficient to note how her clogs are squared off and compare them with the tapering, almost rhythmical design of the footwear that graced Giovannino's figures on the first folios. Various folios follow with representations of poultry and game of notable vivacity, if not great finesse.

Folio 54v, showing a group of peacocks, one displaying an elegant fan-tail, lead us back to the style of the folios in *The Visconti Hours*, with the architectonic setting of the courtyard as well as the design of the figures. But here there is no longer the transfiguring stylishness of the earlier folios but, rather, a quiet housekeeping attitude. A comparison is possible with f. BR-35v in *The Visconti Hours*, where mullioned windows appear (analogous to those represented here) and the borders are decorated with elegant peacocks.

Folio 56 and f. 56v, relative to the preparation of the must, and those immediately following, which concern wines and vinegar, illustrate with delightful realism the various moments dedicated by men and women to tasty and agreeable drinks. The attention is then turned to fish, how it is cooked (f. 59), how it is salted (f. 60), etc. A beautiful counter from which shellfish are sold decorates f. 61.

To substances for sweetening are dedicated f. 62 for sugar and f. 63v for honey, where beehives appear (made of that type of woven straw shown on f. LF-30 in *The Visconti Hours* and drawn by Giovannino). It is notable that, whereas the representation of honey presents analogies with those portraying the same element in other *Tacuina*, that for sugar has no other similarity. In all the other manuscripts a banal shop is shown, whereas here the overloaded baskets, carried by the figure with the wreath on his head, against a background of elegant architecture, achieve a certain graphic success.

Introduced by the beautiful folio with the illustration of roses, f. 64, various others follow, dedicated to moments of life and states of mind, all realized with a courtly taste notwithstanding variations in quality. The result is a complete vision of life "in the round," from the workshop where dresses are sewn (f. 73v) to a scene of dancing (f. 64v); from a moment in a pleasant courtship to that of complete conjugal rapport (f. 69v); in the hunt (f. 72v); in horsemanship (f. 71v); in fencing (f. 72). And illustrations such as the one of the knight seeking shelter from the rain inside the city walls (f. 74v) reveal an affinity for that manner of expression evident in the illustrations of certain fictional works such as *Lancelot* and *Guiron*.

Quite outstanding is the decoration of f. 75, depicting snow and ice, where a dreary landscape is portrayed without the sign of a human presence. I cannot think of any decoration of this type in other manuscripts or even in frescoes of this period. It is a desolate landscape that truly suggests the idea of cold and solitude. Only well into the 1400s will fresco painting offer us landscapes without any human figures, probably one of the earliest examples being that by Masolino in the house of Cardinal Branda Castiglioni, in Castiglione Olona. The "empty" landscape in the Liège *Tacuinum* is probably the starting point for the analogous illustrations in the other *Tacuina*, but only the Casanatense codex offers a similarly barren landscape.

The Paris folio for snow and ice introduces a joyous note by inserting an illustration of a couple throwing snowballs. The Vienna manuscript, in a more subdued mood, presents a small donkey loaded with wood and led by a peasant, almost as if to indicate the way of defending oneself against the cold with a nice small fire. The illustration in the Paris *Tacuinum*, Lat. Ms. 9333, which we are not able to consider here, is also evocative, being particularly indicative in confirming the reference of this work to the German milieu, made by Otto Pächt (1952–53). In the Nordic translation, the absurdity of the small meadow across which the donkey plods laboriously is replaced by the tracks in that snow upon which the animal treads. Instead of green grass, two small, skeletal trees complete the landscape. Nordic logic is substituted for the free play of Italian imagination.

Two folios dedicated to the baths follow—one outdoors in a small lake crowned with fanciful cliffs, the other one indoors. These are illustrations of an absolutely secular taste, drawn with a certain elegance.

Folio 76v shows a ship in full sail on a sea where the waves are slightly agitated and made merrier by the presence of a few fish. The flag bears a cross—could this indicate the manuscript belonged to a member of the Savoy family? Or is it more simply an affirmation of Christianity?

We have seen how important were the ties of kinship among the various ruling families in determining the choice of those artists who were to work on the individual manuscripts. A member of the Savoy family, Bianca, wife of Gian Galeazzo II Visconti, must have played an important part in deciding who would be thusly employed in the Milan area. It was she who selected Giovanni di Benedetto of Como to execute the Book of Hours that is still kept in the Monaco Library. Into the flourishing Milanese workshop were probably channeled commissions from the Savoyard court and, above all, from the Scaligeri as well as the Visconti. Given those strict rapports of kinship, Beatrice Regina della Scala, wife of Bernabò Visconti, must also have played a role of primary importance (in 1381 she dedicated her attention to the construction of the Church of St. Mary of La Scala, for which we would assume she had a Book of Hours illuminated—the Missal Lat. Ms. 757 in the National Library in Paris), and this is truly the keystone for understanding those multiple components at work in the *scriptoria* in Lombardy circa 1380.

The rapport between the French court and the Visconti court is confirmed by the inventory of the trousseau of Valentina Visconti, given in marriage to Louis of Tourraine in 1389, who brought precious manuscripts as well as jewels and embroidered robes. It has not been ascertained that in the proximity of the Savoyard court there were workshops wherein the art of illumination was particularly practiced. It is, therefore, quite plausible that our *Tacuinum* was commissioned by a member of the Savoy House. Those stylistic rapports that indicate the Lombard, Veronese, and transalpine contributions were fundamental components for work done in the Po Valley often find a precise confimation in the exterior histories of the manuscripts.

In various folios the figures, especially those kneeling, reveal a preference for the expression of closed, defined forms that compare precisely with those realized in the Monaco Hours (compare the feminine figure on f. 37v swaddling an infant, in the Monaco manuscript, with the illustrations on f. 24, f. 34, and f. 64 in the Liège manuscript). Architectonical elements that still lead us back to Giovannino's components appear in the folios dedicated to the descriptions of dwellings. Particularly elegant is the arcade in f. 78 supported by slender columns that have the same impalpable grace as those on f. BR-48, f. BR-104v, f. BR-115, or f. BR-35v in *The Visconti Hours*. The mullioned windows, showing the same stylish hand as those on f. BR-1v or f. BR-35v in the same manuscript, are exemplifications of the Lombardian mullioned windows adorning castles such as that in Pavia.

An interest in architecture is a characteristic which dominates the folios in the Liège manuscript, as in no other *Tacuina*. This is an element of determinant importance, in our opinion, in proving that the manuscript came from the same workshop as that which produced *The Visconti Hours* and the *Beroldo*. The round turrets, the fanciful castles, the way of positioning buildings in order to create some internal spaces, that continuous contrapositioning of indoors and outdoors obtained through the use of arcades and ample openings—all these lead us back to the same cultural milieu.

Of particular amplitude are those folios which represent the winds and the four regions among which the earth is divided. This distinction in winds and southern, northern, western, and eastern lands defines precisely the concept of the fixity of the earth whose immobility is mitigated, in a certain sense, by the blowing of the winds, by the variety of climates, and by the changing of the seasons. These are represented by forms that find partial comparisons in the *Tacuina* whose descriptions will follow.

THE "TACUINUM" OF PARIS
—Incunabulum of Courtly Taste

The cultural climate evidenced in the Paris manuscript is obviously quite different from that displayed in the Liège codex. We have seen, in the work of Giovannino dei Grassi, the fundamental matrix of the Liège manuscript, constituting a unique manifestation within the range of Lombardian artistic expression circa 1380 whose documentation, although sufficient to glimpse its importance, is certainly not abundant.

With the Paris manuscript we have a chance to verify in full that eclecticism which had constituted the characteristic element of culture in the Po Valley ever since the early Middle Ages. It is pointless to try to identify the individual hands at work in this manuscript. In 1937, Berti Toesca had already established the presence of several illuminators who had made contributions of varying quality. In our estimation, this is an example of the kind of manuscript which was realized in a workshop by distributing the folios to various artists, in accordance with an overall plan, most probably decided upon collectively. It is without doubt that the most effective accents are the work of those illuminators of pure late Gothic taste who, owing to the complexity of the culture, appear to have been active between 1380 and 1390.

The exterior of the manuscript is not overly helpful in determining the date of its execution. The protective folio that precedes the title-page bears two notes, one of which is of great importance in reconstructing the date. They have been read and transcribed by Berti Toesca—the second one, since it is written in Arabic, with the help of a scholar of Arabic studies, Michelangelo Guido. The first note, in German, allows us to determine that the manuscript once belonged to Verde Visconti, Bernabò's daughter, who married Leopold of Austria (the grandfather of Emperor Frederick III) in 1365. Verde Visconti died in 1405. Therefore, on the basis of these historical elements, the period of the manuscript's realization must have been sometime during those forty years. The note in Arabic informs us that the manuscript had been sent from Smyrna to another location, and underlines the importance of the illustrations. Delisle, who as we have seen in the Introduction was the first to discuss this manuscript (which had become part of the collection of the National Library in Paris in 1891), notes that in several places in the text there are words translated not only in German but also in Czech—from which he deduces that the manuscript remained for some time in a country where this language was spoken.

After a direct comparison of the three manuscripts on display at the 1958 exhibition in Milan, and the imposing photographic campaign derived from it, I believe we may consider this manuscript to antedate the one in Vienna as well as the one in the Casanatense Library in Rome.

Here we are confronted by a culture wherein multiple components are at work, a livelier culture, in a sense. The two other manuscripts I have indicated as being successive will further codify some of its aspects. In those manuscripts a character of great homogeneity will present an expression of a culture totally formed and highly developed, but at its sunset. Arslan too proposes to refer the Paris manuscript to a period preceding the Viennese manuscript, for which he advances a date circa 1390. In his contribution Arslan places the problem of the illuminators' identities in the most modern perspective, that is, by trying to define the fundamental components but leaving a wide margin for "possibilities."

This is also how we will proceed. The highest qualitative expressions appear on the folios where the naturalistic elements constitute the skeletal structure for the representations that present themselves with the modulated and curvilinear cadences typical of flowing Gothic writing. Examples are shown on f. 34, sage; f. 36v, squash; f. 37, sweet melons; f. 37v, tasteless melons; f. 38, Palestinian melons; f. 38v, watermelons and cucumbers; f. 40v, dill. Another group of folios of great interest are those in which Gothic architectural structures of great complexity appear, as on f. 52, barley water; f. 54, white bread; and f. 73v, liver; or naturalistic backgrounds but set with an almost geometric rigor, as in f. 52v, millet, or f. 53, panic grass. These are undoubtedly among the folios which display the most subtle draftsmanship. On a chromatic level, they also evidence a highly developed skill that indulges in the most subtle gradations of color. An exceptional example of this developed French taste is the *"grisaille"* realized on f. 52, barley water. The most successful figures in the Paris manuscript, among which I would include those already mentioned above, are folios such as those illustrating the following elements: f. 46, wheat; f. 47v, barley; f. 48, rice—all of which reveal, as Arslan has already noted, an "expressionistic violence" that is not found in any other Po Valley manuscript.

The problem of the presence in certain folios of the same artistic hand as that which appears in the folios of *Lancelot* and Latin Ms. 757, both of which are in the National Library in Paris (a presence detected by Toesca), seems to us resolvable, as proposed elsewhere, by acknowledging the obvious affinities of certain passages but without referring them all to the Master of the *Lancelot* manuscript, as had been proposed upon the occasion of the Milan exhibition in 1958. It is perhaps more a matter of iconographic convergence than the exact sameness of the artistic hand.

These are, after all, provisional groupings, very useful for a critical study of the works under consideration, that have the merit of allowing the identification of the artistic convergence and, therefore, of clarifying the milieu. It is perhaps difficult to emphasize sufficiently how recent is that photographic development which makes it possible for us to study various works simultaneously, and in great detail, thus being able to proceed with a precise comparison with a memory-aid in our hands.

One must also keep in mind that trend of studies centered, above all as far as painting is concerned, on the search for attribution based on a critical line connected to criteria of pure visibility. Critical honesty demands I state that this methodology had already been discarded by the school of Paolo d'Ancona, and sometimes I ask myself whether it was not precisely his preference for studies centered upon the illuminations which gave him that amplitude of vision in accordance with which attribution became an element among the many that constituted a philological definition, and nothing more. But during those years Italian art criticism was polarized, after all, by the quality of Longhi's reconstructions, and one had to leave Italy in order to find those works he had rejected held elsewhere in great esteem. It is sufficient to remember the book *The Court of Lodovico the Moor* by Malaguzzi Valeri, dismissed by one of Longhi's reviews, which Pellegrin, however, has judged to be, together with Toesca's studies, among the most important of all works dedicated to illumination. It was probably Longhi's considerable influence which induced certain attributions at the time of the Milan Exhibition of Lombard art, without considering the difference in the situation proposed by the illuminated manuscripts vis-à-vis that of paintings. It involves a substantial difference in execution. A folio was often (but not always) executed by one artist, while one hundred or two hundred "paintings" (which is not an exceptional number in a manuscript) were executed in a workshop through a distribution of the folios, often in accordance with the technical necessity of their successive binding into a book. The history of illumination, which is still often defined as a "minor art" and, consequently, studied according to canons that were used in the study of the "major art" of painting, will most likely have to be reconsidered, as Porcher has correctly proposed, as the fundamental lens for a real understanding of medieval painting. It is a reversal of terms and emphasis.

These considerations allow us to look with an autonomy of judgment not possible before upon the folios of our manuscripts and to admire the readiness with which the various illuminators passed on certain basic outlines to each other. Thus, the figures leaning out from balconies that appear similar in certain folios—for example, in that for horseback riding and on various pages of the *Lancelot* and Latin Ms. 757—may represent the evidence of the same artist at work, or indicate the approach to certain artistic problems which typified the production of a particular workshop.

The first folio of the Paris manuscript shows, as do those in the other *Tacuina*, a man sitting at his desk (in this case, the chair is a typically Gothic flowery throne, sketched with lines typical of the Po Valley manuscripts). It is worthwhile to consider this representation in a comparative manner, as related to fresco paintings of the 1300s. This representation by an ample design has indeed a fresco dimension. Folio 1 is the only one which presents this relationship, and we may consider it as having been executed by an artist who did not work on the other folios of the manuscript.

As we continue to leaf through the manuscript, we become aware of the fact that the transition from the painter's activity to that of the illuminator's and vice-versa, must have been more common than scholarship thus far has been able to determine.

A common characteristic of the major number of folios in the manuscript is the combined presence of a lady and a knight who appear so absorbed in a dialogue that the specific element represented seems only a pretext for the illustration of their interpersonal rapport. This characteristic is evident in the Paris *Tacuinum* only, and it accentuates the courtly character of the manuscript, rather than that of a medical book of prescriptions. As the novels *Lancelot* and *Guiron* narrate knightly exploits, here the figurative part of the manuscript seems to illustrate and emphasize a couple's rapport (with other moments inserted that are connected to other presences).

For example, a very lively scene is that showing two mischievous urchins who play games while operating the grape press (f. 76). A moment of tranquillity is represented on the page dedicated to chatting (f. 90). Fragments of life are illustrated on many folios, such as the little scene on f. 46 (chick pea soup), where we see an old man who is receiving a cup of broth that has been prepared over the fire by a girl dressed in a graphically Gothic manner typical of Giovannino dei Grassi's workshop. But the cup of broth is passed to a footman, an obvious pretext for another graphic insert (note his footwear and clothing), and, successively, to an elegant woman who hands it to the old man with a gentle gesture. Representations that illustrate these dialectical passages are not uncommon in this manuscript and constitute, in part, its particular charm.

The baking of bread (f. 55, f. 55v, and f. 56), the milking of sheep (f. 56v), the preparation of cheese, specifically ricotta (f. 58v, f. 59v, and f. 59), the gathering of eggs in the poultry pen in the presence of two engaging roosters (f. 60), the various moments of butchering different types of cattle (f. 61v, f. 62, f. 62v, f. 63, f. 63v and others), and many additional aspects of man's daily toiling find in the illustrations of this manuscript their liveliest interpretations.

It appears unquestionable that works such as the Liège *Tacuinum* constituted an important precedent to the Paris codex. We would even be tempted to attribute to the Liège manuscript the function of prototype. And there are two reasons for this: the vitality of all its folios, which is typical of an original work, and the manner of its execution.

As we have noted when considering the various folios, we are not, strictly speaking, dealing with illuminations in the Liège manuscript, but rather with drawings and the addition of color where naturalistic representation demanded it. A shred of doubt also remains as to when the color was added. Drawing is, by its very nature, the first and most immediate graphic translation of artistic expression. The immediacy of the representations in the Liège manuscript could have aroused in more than one patron the desire for a illuminated rendition, of undoubtedly greater pretension.

The difference between a drawing that the artist does as an end in itself and one conceived as a support for the successive phase of illumination is an enormous one. It is enough to observe some pages of those illuminated manuscripts whose decoration, for whatever reasons, was interrupted, to immediately become aware of this difference.

But even if we wish to recognize in the Liège manuscript, in a certain sense, the prototype for the *Tacuina* we are considering here, and perhaps, for others that will be found successively, the problem concerning the source of these figures remains a subject for discussion. We have already referred to this in the Introduction, when we proposed to share Otto Pächt's critical indication, which was advanced in his fundamental contribution of 1950.

In order to understand this desire to reproduce through images the offerings of Nature from which men can derive benefit or injury, we may return to the illustrations in the classic texts such as that of *Dioscoride's* medical treatise, known to us from the famous manuscript now in the National Library in Vienna, which was executed circa 512. The illustrations of herbs are exceptionally vivid in this manuscript and there is a striving for realistic immediacy which is singularly effective.

This concentration upon representations that give a clear picture of how herbs, small plants, etc., appear in nature reappears after the closing of that great parenthesis of Byzantium, a period during which all representations had been conveyed by way of abstractions, in manuscripts such as the one in Lucca, mentioned above, and in other herbal manuals for medical use from Salerno, such as Ms. K.IV.3 in the National Library in Turin, written in the twelfth century, according to Giacosa, with the style of Cassino, or the prescription book (Ms. Vari 129) in the Royal Library in Turin.

Otto Pächt points to the particularly significant codex in the British Museum, Egerton Ms. 747, as the prototype for the illustrated *Secreta Salernitana*. We agree with this scholar in considering the Florentine manuscript Pal. 586 as being a shortened version derived from the herbal manuals in alphabetical order in the group of *Secreta Salernitana* but not the first illustrated example of *Tacuinum Sanitatis*. Therefore we may consider it a link but not a prototype, although very interesting indeed, because it introduces us to a climate typically Gothic. The decoration of the manuscript was presumably done in Southern France and was accomplished in two phases (although it remained unfinished), presumably toward the middle of the fourteenth century.

An important indication in the evaluation of the scientific-naturalistic spirit that inspired the realization of the Salerno manuals on herbs is that we can discern in certain representations that the leaf of the plant in question was placed on the paper and a drawing in outline thus realized. We shall have to wait until the end of the fifteenth century before the same dried plant will be substituted for a freehand drawing in the composition of manuals on herbs.

Therefore, we may say that from the medieval manuals on herbs was derived a literary form (that of the *Tacuina*) and a scientific form (that of herbal manuals intended in a modern sense). Thus, on one hand, we have illuminated codices containing precepts of good health for a rarified world that could afford to own a book made to order; on the other hand, naturalistic collections that will eventually flow into Botanical Institutes. Among the latter perhaps the most ancient is that once owned by Ulisse Aldovrandi in the second half of the sixteenth century, with 1,347 individual entries, now a part of the collection of the Botanical Institute of Bologna.

From these codices, whether illuminated or not, will be derived the printed editions. In the case of our manuscripts the complete Arabic text by Ibn Botlân, translated into Latin, will serve as the source for the 1531 edition with wood engravings by Jean Schott, printer of Strasbourg, dedicated to Albert of Brandenburg, and the following edition published in 1533 in German. It is important to notice how, from a common medieval matrix on the threshold of the modern era, two veins sprang into being—one of which we may call humanistic and the other scientific. We are at the moment when two ways of investigating creation begin to take shape.

That the Arab culture, after having taken into consideration classic texts such as that of *Dioscoride* (whose illustrated Arabic translation we have mentioned) together with its own texts, came to represent an important foundation for medieval universities is without doubt—it is somewhat more surprising to think that the courtly illustrations in the Paris *Tacuinum* find their justification, in part, in the diffusion of the precepts of Arabic medicine in the West.

THE "TACUINUM" OF VIENNA

The manuscript in Vienna was the first of the *Tacuina* to be subjected to a detailed study. It was discussed by Schlosser in that periodical which listed the works owned by the Imperial House but which, in practice, served Viennese scholarship of the times as a vehicle for the definition of certain fundamental problems concerning the figurative arts. The periodical began publication in 1883, and these were very vital years for Middle European culture as centered in the Viennese area.

Schlosser's article concerning the Vienna manuscript appeared in 1895. In this article the scholar proposed the attribution of the manuscript to the Verona milieu on the basis of two fundamental arguments: stylistic analysis, strengthened by the external consideration that he thought the codex belonged to the Cerruti family of Verona (indicating that he recognized their coat of arms on f. 3v). Since 1905, however, this identification has been questioned by valid arguments put forward by Muñoz.

The other coat of arms contained in the manuscript on f. 1v, which had not been identified by Schlosser, was subsequently identified by Kurth (in 1911) as belonging to George of Lichtenstein, who was Bishop of Trent from 1390 to 1419. But he must have been in possession of the manuscript before 1407, since it was during that year that he left Trent, never to return. He evidently did not take the manuscript with him since it was most probably this codex, under the listing of "*Herbalarium cum figuris pictis,*" which appeared as part of the inventory ordered by Duke Frederick of the Tyrol in 1410.

The successive history of the manuscript is well known up until 1936, when it became part of the collection of the Austrian National Library in Vienna, but this latter part of its history is of only slight interest to any critical study of the manuscript, whereas the indications that point toward George of Lichtenstein are of substantial importance.

These indications lead us back to Trent where, during the years from 1400 to

1407, one of the most stunningly beautiful series of courtly decorations ever painted on a wall was realized: the frescoes in the hall of the *Torre dell' Aquila* near the *Castello del Buonconsiglio* in Trent. As early as 1905, Fogolari had noted a rapport between the Vienna manuscript and the decoration of this hall. Concerning the latter's origin he had initially expressed some doubt that it was done by a German painter rather than an Italian, but he eventually concluded by emphasizing those components in the frescoes that point toward the Veronese milieu. Fogolari's conclusions were truly enlightened, since they contained, in a nutshell, all that scholarship would later elaborate upon. He had also noted the general concordance between the frescoes in Trent depicting the Cycle of the Months and the portrayal of the succession of the seasons (with their influence upon agricultural efforts) as illustrated in manuscripts realized beyond the Alps, such as the famous *Très Riches Heures of Jean, Duke of Berry*. (In the Trent frescoes, however, the mowing of hay is shown as taking place somewhat later, in July, and the harvesting of wheat in August.) Fogolari's conclusion that there was a rapport between the *Tacuinum* and the frescoed cycle in Trent precedes the discovery, in 1911, that the manuscript had belonged to the same Bishop of Trent who also had commissioned the frescoes. Undoubtedly, the manuscript was realized before the frescoes—we think the hypothesis that it was executed for the same George of Lichtenstein soon after he was elevated to the rank of Bishop, therefore immediately after 1390, should not be discounted. It is also probable that the prelate turned to an artist already active during that period at the Courts of the Visconti or the Scaligeri.

In this connection, the following argument put forward by Rasmo in 1972 (with which we agree) should not be underestimated:

> Painters and illuminators at work in feudal courts, whether large or small, constituted a separate category of specialists generally exempt from the discipline of the increasingly powerful artisan guilds in the towns, since they were considered recognized members of the court, or else they traveled from castle to castle in the service of various nobles, and were also exempt from the norms governing town life.

Thus, on the basis of personal rapports, a Bishop's request for the execution of a manuscript is understandable. We might even hypothesize that the desire to possess this type of work may have been aroused in him by knowledge of the precious *Tacuinum* owned by Verde Visconti, wife of Duke Leopold of Austria (we have seen that this manuscript should be considered as having been executed previously, on the basis of its stylistic characteristics).

The concordance between the Vienna *Tacuinum* and the frescoes (noted by all the scholars who have studied both, including Fogolari, Morassi, and Rasmo) could also be explained differently. The hypothesis that the frescoes in the *Torre dell' Aquila* were the work of a Bohemian artist, established by Rasmo through the identification of Master Venceslao, "eclectic, evidently of Nordic formation, probably originating from somewhere in the marginal region of Bohemia between Prague and Vienna," leads us back to that same milieu from which came many important stimuli for the culture of the Po Valley.

We have seen that, in our opinion, it is exactly within a Bohemian milieu that a search must be conducted in order to clarify the question of the formation of Giovannino dei Grassi. Now, in the Northern Italian culture, whether we wish to define it as being of the Po Valley in accordance with a terminology embracing a vaster set of possibilities, or more precisely Lombardian in accordance with a narrower focus, a fundamental stimulation undoubtedly stemmed from the multiform personality of Giovannino dei Grassi, a presence of determinant value for any workshop of stonecutters or illuminators, most likely because of the diffusion of his drawings throughout the various workshops for use in their repertoires. To such a culture must be linked the execution of that manuscript which once belonged to the Bishop of Trent. We can thus glimpse some constant rapports of give-and-take between the Bohemian milieu and that of the Po Valley, as defined through the study of the works still extant.

A reconstruction of the history of the manuscripts, with the aim of pinpointing in the manuscript now in Paris the incentive for a later realization such as that presently in Vienna, is an extension of the dialogue which began between Schlosser and Delisle when the latter, in 1886 (a year after Schlosser's article), compared the two manuscripts for the first time. The rapports between these manuscripts are undeniable, but by referring to those folios studied and compared by Delisle, together with the recognizable similarity of the iconography, it is natural to note how different are the problems presented by each manuscript.

The illustrations mentioned by Delisle are: turnips, f. 43; spelt, f. 48v; wheat pasta, f. 50; ricotta, f. 59; partridges, f. 67v; theriac, f. 87v; vomit, f. 89; autumn, f. 103v. In all of these folios we find minor figurative dynamics present in the Vienna manuscript—a dimension indicating the inward turning of a culture. The dialogue between the two people shown on f. 51 (turnips) in the Paris manuscript is enlivened through the sinuous line of that Gothic style which imparts a certain liveliness to the folio, accentuated by the irregular modulation of the blossoming meadow and of the stylized plant (which visually interrupts the dialogue between the man and woman) around whose stem a climber, as indicated by its pointed "Gothic" leaves, is clambering up. The folio in the Vienna manuscript for this same element has translated everything that is dynamic in the Paris manuscript into rigid forms. The terrain displays an almost geometric regularity. From it rise some small plants, also laid out geometrically. The feminine figure is engrossed, almost absent-mindedly, being only an affected shadow of those damsels drawn by Giovannino dei Grassi on the folios of *The Visconti Hours*. The male figure displays the same heavy step as that depicted in an analogous representation on f. 215v of the *Historia Plantarum*.

Similar considerations are prompted by the comparison between the spelt folios (f. 48v, Paris; f. 47, Vienna). Besides the fact (which applies to all folios in these manuscripts) that the dimension of the part reserved for illustrations is greater in the Paris manuscript and of a markedly more rectangular shape, the entire effect is completely different. That which, in the Paris manuscript, shows a vivacious little rural scene representing the rapport between a knight and his horse has been transformed, in the Vienna manuscript, into a nonindividualized scene.

The homey character of the folios that show women busy preparing noodles (wheat pasta—f. 50, Paris; f. 45v, Vienna) is depicted in a very different manner in each of the two manuscripts. As always in the Paris manuscript, the interest is centered upon the rapport of collaboration that unites the two women busily engaged in their work, which they perform with vivacious gestures. The folio in the Vienna manuscript expresses something akin to the boredom of repeating a usual gesture.

Analogous considerations apply to the other folios. There always emerges, even in the identity of the subject represented, an obvious difference in cultural climate. The folio dedicated to the preparation of ricotta (f. 59, Paris; f. 62, Vienna), which in the Paris manuscript is set in the kitchen of an aristocratic residence, takes place in a humble hut in the Vienna manuscript. In both folios we are very far from the immediacy of representation that had characterized the drawings in the Liège codex.

In order to see the problem in terms of a sociological interpretation of art, we might note that whoever was responsible for the coordination of the illuminators' work in the Paris manuscript had a vision of the world filtered through courtly life, so that even the humblest kind of work becomes the pretext for a refined and elegant depiction. In the Vienna manuscript daily toil is represented with greater fidelity to everyday life, even if the central point of reference always remains that of court life or, if one prefers, palace life. These are rarefied worlds, however, from which any hint of pain or suffering is deliberately excluded, and whose dimension of reality is centered upon the constant preoccupation with maintaining that man-nature rapport so evident in almost every folio.

Professor Unterkircher has recently undertaken a complete study of the Vienna *Tacuinum* as an introduction to the reproduction of the manuscript in facsimile. He distinguishes the presence of two artists—recognizing, however, that the conception of the whole is essentially unitary, due to the overall design being the work of a single illuminator. We are in full agreement here. A total homogeneity of vision, in fact, represents the fundamental character of this work. In examining other manuscripts of the same type, very rarely do we detect an analogous coherence. We are less sure about there having been only one additional artist who collaborated in the decoration of the manuscript. Furthermore, the localization of that intervention as having taken place on f. 88 through f. 95v appears too confining to us.

There is undoubtedly a difference in the rigid style of the illuminator who worked on f. 77v (yellow-colored wine) and the one who drew, with such an expression of free fantasy and certainty, the lines on f. 88 (salt water), one of the most important folios in the entire manuscript. I have already had occasion to note that this is one of the plates that confirms better than any other the thesis of the Venetian derivation of the manuscript. When compared with the page facing the title-page of *De Viris Illustribus* by Petrarch, Ms. Lat. 6069 in the National

Library in Paris, the analogy of the cultural climate is evident. Petrarch's manuscript was composed in 1380 at Padua for Francesco da Carrara by Lombardo della Seta, Petrarch's disciple.

The indication of this Venetian derivation is further confirmed by Pallucchini who defined the rapport of this configuration with the *Miracle of St. Mark* by Paolo Veneziano. This illuminator, whose Venetian connotations appear evident to us, may be the very same artist who painted the light, elegant plates, f. 89, warm water, or f. 91, oil of almonds, but is not to be identified with the artist who worked on f. 90, snow and ice, who reveals in his landscape a volumetric definition that would have been considered discordant within the Venetian milieu, and displays in his figure a rigid folding of the drapery that is very far from the quivering brushwork evident not only on f. 89 and f. 91 but also on f. 92, sugar, and elsewhere.

We think the work of another assistant is concealed among the folios of the Vienna manuscript, one who must have worked on *Historia Plantarum*, Ms. 459 in the Casanatense Library in Rome (which, in our opinion, came from the workshop of Giovannino dei Grassi, but without his personal intervention). We mention f. 255v in the Roman codex, in comparison with f. 39, violets, or f. 52v, turnips, where the rapport is not only iconographic, in the sense that plants are always represented whose sprouting leaves offer a certain analogy, but is also determined by the insertion of the human figure that thus integrates the composition, blending with the naturalistic illustration. Folio 54v in the *Historia Plantarum* also presents an analogous situation and can be compared with a folio such as f. 48v, sorghum, if we wish to advance the thesis of an identity of execution; but the same thing applies to many other plates, such as f. 47v and f. 48, millet and panic grass, if we wish to limit ourselves to a comparison of similar compositions. We have already underlined the correspondence of execution between f. 215v and f. 51, turnips; we would also like to advance the same connection between f. 140 and f. 63v, coagulated milk, in the Vienna manuscript.

Leafing through the manuscript, the similarities apparent are further defined within that character of homogeneity which, in agreement with Unterkircher, we have recognized. Folio 54, summer, undoubtedly one of the most delicate in the entire manuscript, should now be reconsidered in the light of the analysis of the Liège manuscript which has been published here for the first time. The Vienna composition has as its matrix the two folios (f. 81, summer, and f. 28, wheat) in the Liège codex. Upon close scrutiny, the composition of the scene evidences, in fact, two distinct visual moments, graphically defined in a certain sense by the small, centrally placed tree. Here, Giovannino's matrix, gathered through the repertoires, is evident and, notwithstanding the transcription, remains as the very appropriate background for the whole composition.

As far as the Paris *Tacuinum* is concerned, we have hypothesized that it was precisely the awareness of this manuscript which prompted the Bishop of Trent to seek to have a similar work done for him; but this does not prove that the illuminator commissioned with its execution had in *his* hands the codex once owned by Verde Visconti. Among other things, the rapport between George of Lichtenstein and the Imperial House of Austria was not the best; therefore, we do not feel we can state with certainty (as does Professor Unterkircher) that the Paris *Tacuinum* served the function of model.

With the expansion of knowledge and—let us state it frankly—the diffusion of photography (which is not yet a century old), we must accustom ourselves to a more flexible interpretation of works of art and begin to accept the fact that a relationship, apparently direct and peremptory, may have actually been the result of multiple mediations. Knowledge of the Liège *Tacuinum*, for example, does alter the situation. The rapport of the manuscript with the great fresco painting in Trent, first defined by Fogolari, finds particular confirmation in some folios that were in all probability closely studied by the fresco painter himself. Note the folio with the representation of spring, f. 55v, which is significant when one compares it to the representation of the Month of May in the Cycle of the Months fresco. Rasmo underlined the presence in Trent, at the end of 1300, of painters originally from Lombardy; the Vienna *Tacuinum* probably contributed to the defining of that cultural climate which welcomed the Master invited by George of Lichtenstein (in all probability, that Venceslao of Bohemian extraction identified by Rasmo).

THE "THEATRUM" IN THE
CASANATENSE LIBRARY IN ROME

In contrast to the Paris and Vienna manuscripts, we cannot attempt to date the Casanatense codex with any real degree of accuracy. Nevertheless, its stylistic characteristics and rapport with the Vienna *Tacuinum* lead us to hypothesize that it may have been completed toward the end of the 1300s. We think this is a reasonable assumption in accordance with the observable characteristics of the folios which would seem to have been the work of various illuminators influenced by Giovannino dei Grassi, perhaps even members of his own workshop (from which emerged another original Casanatense manuscript, the *Historia Plantarum*, mentioned above).

On the other hand, there are no signs that might indicate a familiarity with the work of another great Lombard illuminator, Michelino da Besozzo, who in 1402, although certainly still young, was already an artist of such renown that he was assigned the illumination of the funeral oration by Pietro da Castelletto for Gian Galeazzo Visconti. The fluid line of Michelino, who never displayed any of the expressionistic traits of Giovannino dei Grassi, imposed a different style upon the Lombard workshops—a style which influenced even minor personalities. The figures in the Casanatense codex, however, appear entirely free of his influence.

We are confronted with a manuscript emerging from a well-established school where the success of the pagination was the fruit of long experience. The precedents are those already noted for the other manuscripts, and they range from the medieval manuals on herbs to the multiple artistic components of late Gothic culture. It is that very same eclectic climate that witnessed the confluence of the most vital Middle European experiences which were channeled into the workshop operating for the Duomo of Milan and the Certosa of Pavia. This, undoubtedly, was the climate wherein Giovannino dei Grassi excelled. But we would like to specify that the character of this manuscript is the same as that evident in the *Historia Plantarum* in the same Casanatense Library, rather than the *Beroldo* manuscript, which has also been linked to Giovannino and which was executed at about the end of the 1300s.

In order to interpret the twofold indications revealed on one side by the two Casanatense manuscripts and, on the other side, by the *Beroldo* codex, we must return to the multiform personality of Giovannino dei Grassi, as it was expressed in the work which emerged during the three decades his presence was detectable in the Milan area. From the stupendous folios in *The Visconti Hours* (which, as we have seen, was probably begun in 1370) a twofold trend in illumination springs into being. The one that can be traced back more directly to Giovannino is contained in the *Beroldo* manuscript (still kept in the Trivulziana Library in Milan) and was realized during the last years of Giovannino's life—the payment for this manuscript being made to his son Salomone in 1398, after Giovannino's death.

The last ten years of the 1300s saw Giovannino engaged primarily as *capo-maestro* for the Duomo. This preoccupation with architectonic realization permeates the pages of the *Beroldo* manuscript and constitutes the factor unifying all of its illustrations. This vital interest in architecture is not identifiable in the other trend of illumination that also leads back to Giovannino (as validated by the two Casanatense codices which do not show, however, any intervention by his hand. These are, moreover, further removed from the realizations in the Duomo of Milan).

In the *Historia Plantarum* Giovannino's school displays the master's imprint, above all through that interest in the human figure and in animals which was typical of Giovannino's work in the first folios he did for *The Visconti Hours* and was certainly transmitted by him through drawings such as those in the prestigious Bergamo drawing book. The confluence of the representations in the *Historia Plantarum* and the *Theatrum Sanitatis* are evident and have already been discussed in previous studies (for example, more than one configuration in the *Theatrum* is linked, iconographically, to the images in the *Historia Plantarum*). But at this point, we have reached the last translations of Giovannino's vibrant images. The workshop from which the Casanatense manuscript emerged certainly found in Giovannino its first matrix but successively moved away from it in subsequent executions.

No architectonic notation in the *Theatrum* evidences the extraordinary vitality of the steeple painted in the lower right-hand margin of f. 1 in the Beroldo manuscript. It also does not indicate the milieu which we see bubbling with life on that same f. 1 in the architectonic insertion of St. Augustine's baptism, reminiscent of the liveliest achievements of Lombard culture in 1380 (visible at its highest levels in manuscripts such as the Book of Hours, Missal, Lat. 757, in the National Library in Paris, which provided the true keystone for the knowledge of the Lombard milieu of that period).

The indication at the beginning of the *Theatrum* (no longer *Tacuinum*) *Sanitatis* reinforces in a certain sense that feeling of lessened vitality vis-à-vis the other manuscripts under consideration which is verifiable on each folio of the *Theatrum*. The architectonic element which had been determinant (above all in the Paris manuscript) is almost entirely absent. The immediacy of the depictions of home life in the Vienna manuscript gives way here to a more contained representation. With this statement we do not wish to disparage the charm of the manuscript but rather to define its character, which is centered primarily upon the multiple aspects of nature as descriptively perceived. It is a more placid psychological dimension that pervades the manuscript. This becomes a work to be considered primarily through the illustrations, i e., to be "looked at" (we refer here to the Greek etymology of the word *theatrum*), but also a work which shares less in life's more immediate aspects. Indicative in this sense is the scene illustrating anger, f. cxc. The folio in the Casanatense manuscript was evidently derived from f. 98v in the Vienna codex, but the elimination of naturalistic elements emphasizes its more emblematic character and depersonalizes it. We are very far from the impact of the Liège illustration, where a woman is tearing at the clothes across her bosom, her face contorted in an effectively expressive grimace (f. 66).

The strict rapport between the Vienna codex and this manuscript in the Casanatense Library had already been uniformly agreed upon by scholars after the first articles published in 1905 by Fogolari, who had already defined the situation by stating that the manuscript "is close to the Paris manuscript in its text and a copy of the Vienna manuscript in its illustrations." Rather than a copy, we might say that it was derived from the Vienna manuscript but has particular characteristics of its own.

The first indication is that human figures are not so much in evidence. That sort of discursive rapport among individuals, relevant in the Paris manuscript, already less accentuated in the Vienna manuscript (but still present), becomes even rarer in the Casanatense manuscript. It is a return, in a certain sense, to the intent of the original manuals on herbs aimed at constituting a memory-aid by depicting particular plants. Thus the folios dedicated to the naturalistic representations point out with particular efficacy the botanical aspect of the illustration in question. But here the intention is also to provide a memory-aid for life as lived. The botanical aspect is accentuated, but with a different emphasis—one that we may define as medico-philosophical. The difference in climate as compared to the Vienna *Tacuinum* (which is undoubtedly the one closest to the *Theatrum*) lies exactly in this ulterior indication of a late Gothic sense which leads to an intellectualized definition of reality that finds no counterpart in the immediacy of the Vienna folios.

If it has been of fundamental importance for scholars to define the iconographical affinities of these two codices (as well as for the others also under consideration), it appears equally important today, now that they have been systematized, to examine them within a larger dimension and define the differences in cultural climate that five manuscripts such as our *Tacuina* can clarify through the vivid presence of their illustrations. A manifold study of reality results, a reality which, having as its starting point the achievements of that medieval period often considered indicative of a moment when faith in transcendental values conferred a certain stability upon life, suddenly gives way to an obvious multiplicity of interpretations.

This life and its various aspects—especially in its adherence to nature—is revealed on folios such as the one used to illustrate sour cherries (f. xvii). The folio for this element is chromatically very effective in the Vienna codex, and a particular vitality is also maintained in the simplified Casanatense version. This is so even though only the figure of a youngster busy gathering fruit appears here. The two courteous, elegant damsels in the Vienna *Tacuinum* (one of whom is departing with two full baskets balanced on her shoulders) have been eliminated in the Casanatense rendering. And the terrain, which is still drawn with an eye toward that typical rhythm used to graphically define the furrow, is more schematically represented. The illustration of the same subject in the Rouen codex will further accentuate the naturalistic aspect, and the small figure of the youngster will almost seem to blend with the branches of the tree.

The rapport between the folio in the Vienna manuscript and that in the Casanatense codex for the illustration of fennel (f. lxxvi) is quite evident. The male figure (dressed in red in the Casanatense version) is of particular chromatic efficacy; but the tendency here is still toward a graphic simplification. The small trees rising above the shrubs in the Vienna version have been eliminated here. We are very far removed from the version in the Liège codex (f. 22v), where the naturalistic aspect of the folio constituted a pretext for delineating a first meeting between two young people against the background of a castle within a fanciful landscape. The Paris illustration was also to be interpreted in this sense.

The folio representing wheat (f. lxxviii) is among the most evocative in the manuscript. The golden crop bends lightly beneath the soft breeze, without any trace of a human presence. The toiling and hard work seem to have been forgotten, whereas they are very evident in the Liège (f. 28) and the Paris (f. 46v) manuscripts; in the Vienna codex (f. 42v) the human presence is merely an insert. Thus the depiction here, even in the reality of the subject represented, is fundamentally symbolic. In a different cultural moment, it could have indicated the passage toward the most absolute abstraction (we are thinking here of Mondrian's tree).

Analogous considerations are valid for f. lxxxviii, millet, but it is worthwhile to underline the vitality of this culture which, in the passing of less than twenty years (the period, in our opinion, that elapsed between the production of the Liège *Tacuinum* and the Casanatense codex), was responsible for inspiring works that evidence such a diverse way of conceiving and depicting life. Folio 31 in the Liège manuscript is one of the most densely populated of all the illustrations, and it teems with life: in a fanciful landscape dominated by the usual castle rising almost as if by incantation upon a steep cliff (typical of work derived from Giovannino dei Grassi's inspiration), a man and a woman flail the small grains while a hen with its brood of chicks awaits the grain, and two oxen appear intent upon other work. Folio 52v in the Paris manuscript, as we have noted previously, is one of the most significant in linking that manuscript to a milieu of refined Gothic taste, whereas, as filtered through the version in the Vienna codex, the Casanatense folio evidences the usual and intentional absence of other elements, resulting in an intellectual accentuation of the naturalistic aspect.

Folio cxxviii, partridges, is distinctly derived from the folio which appears in the Vienna manuscript. Since it is also chromatically similar, we think it might have been done by the same rather modest illuminator, sensitive to the courtly taste of the times even if superficially interpreted. There is a noticeable discrepancy between a folio such as this and the folio used to illustrate wheat in the same manuscript.

Folio lxxxii, *savich* or barley soup, is to be linked to the Vienna folio for the same element, although the composition is reversed here. It is still a typical representation of an indoor scene of noteworthy efficacy. Clearly, however, the exquisite grace of the Liège drawing (f. 34, with the girl bending over the hearthstone, intent upon the preparation of the barley meal) does not appear here.

Folio lxviii, sage, differs noticeably from all those in the other manuscripts. It is a particularly effective illustration in every version. Here, the composition has changed —there is only one female figure with a large basket gathering the sage—whereas in the Vienna codex the composition was symmetrical. The Paris folio was considered by Arslan (whose opinion we share) "an illustrious example" among the miniatures of a master more distinctly "Lombardian" in his executions. In this version the two women who gather the sage in their ample skirts, held up by both ends in such a way as to form a concave space, do so with a supple movement that unifies them rhythmically with the dense foliage. The Liège drawing (f. 16) for the same subject is one of the folios in that manuscript wherein architectonic interest appears more evident, and the entire composition centered upon the small green plants is particularly effective.

Sweet milk (f. cxi) is one of the illustrations which were compared by Serra to analogous ones in the *Historia Plantarum;* the rapport is undeniable, as Toesca has already noted, when referring to f. 55 and f. 83 in this manuscript. I would be tempted to recognize in the Liège illustration on f. 37v the first matrix for the sweet-milk illustration in the Vienna manuscript (f. 59), the Paris manuscript (f. 57), and in the Casanatense codex (f. cxi). But careful study of this illustration persuades us that here too we are not dealing with an original work. The folio was certainly derived from a matrix of Giovannino's but as adapted by his workshop. (Incontestable evidence of this is provided by the edges of the rock, which display a certain awkwardness.)

The woman busy cooking on f. 95v of the *Historia Plantarum*, whose likeness to the woman shown in the illustrations on f. LXXX, barley soup, and f. CXLIV, roasted meat, was correctly detected by Serra, finds a correspondence in the same illustration in the Vienna manuscript (f. 43v, barley soup; f. 75v, roasted meat), but also in those on f. 64, ricotta, as well as in the kneeling figure on f. 66, goose eggs (in this illustration, the comparison is so definite in the way of draping the gown as to allow the supposition that the drawing was done by the same artist), and on f. 81, entrails or tripe. The folio with the illustration of roses, f. LXIX, differs noticeably from those in the other manuscripts and reveals the hand of an illuminator of consummate artistry, as evidenced by the effective compositional balance and the wisdom of the chromatic interplay. The open codex, in which this folio faces the one done for sage (by the same illuminator), seems to provide evidence of two different compositional approaches in the manuscript—one defined by symmetry (roses), and the other by asymmetry (sage). These facing pages are the most successful matches of all the folios in the codex. The Vienna *Tacuinum* presents the same situation, but both illustrations exhibit the usual symmetry as interpreted by an illuminator of lesser capacity. The Paris version moves in a different direction altogether, and presents the usual discursive rapport between two people (around which, as we have seen, the decoration of a good part of the codex revolves). It is possible that the first matrix of the illustration of the roses might have been the one which came to light in the Liège drawing. Folio 64 in that manuscript is one of rare efficacy, and the four women busy around the tree lead us unerringly to the exquisite female figures in the small Bergamo drawing book and to *The Visconti Hours*, both by Giovannino dei Grassi.

Folio LXXXVII, spelt, composed symmetrically in contraposition to the illustration for rye on the preceding folio, might be reminiscent of the folio for rye in the Liège *Tacuinum* (f. 28v) and is certainly to be considered in relation to f. 44, barley, in the Vienna codex, to which it surely corresponds and with which it shares the same successful golden tonality. (In examining these folios, the acknowledgment of the sure existence of repertoires in the workshops finds further confirmation.) The figure of the harvester busy with the reaping, using a sickle, that appears on the folio for wheat (f. 28) in Liège is analogous to f. 46v, rye, and f. 54, summer, in the Vienna codex and to f. LXXXVI, rye, in the Casanatense manuscript, not to mention other correspondences less definite, such as f. 46v (wheat) in the Paris Codex.

The illustrations of the seasons are precisely related in both the Casanatense and Vienna manuscripts. We have already noted with regard to the folio for summer in the Vienna *Tacuinum* the influence of Giovannino dei Grassi. An analogous consideration applies to the Casanatense folio. In the folios illustrating autumn, a sharper naturalism is detectable in both codices. The folio dedicated to winter shows a greater liveliness in the Vienna manuscript. It is a typical representation of indoors both in this manuscript and in the less successful Casanatense version. These indoor scenes, so frequent in our *Tacuina*, undoubtedly constitute the most exact depiction of the life of the period. Before our eyes, delightful little scenes unfold of life as lived in the shops and in the houses. We arrive at illustrations of unprejudiced realism such as that for coitus, f. cxcvi in the Casanatense codex, f. 100v in the Paris manuscript, and f. 69v in the Liège *Tacuinum* (this being the liveliest of all). The folio for this activity has been removed from the Vienna manuscript.

The overall impression of *Theatrum Sanitatis* is analogous to that offered by the Vienna *Tacuinum*, notwithstanding the differences in background already noted. The text also presents a similarity in its layout and design. It has approximately the same dimensions (whereas that of Paris is shortened), and it is preceded by an introductory note that is omitted in both the Paris and Liège manuscripts. It is the typical codex that must have enjoyed great success among those free to partake of the leisure of courtly living—eager to be informed, but averse to demanding reading. Folio cIV, spring, typically courtly in its layout, offers the synthesis of this disengaged life. Noblemen and noblewomen converse amiably in a delightful garden in full bloom, among small birds fluttering amidst the trees. The serenity of the scene constitutes its dominant note. It springs spontaneously to mind that no other representation of the period defines with equal efficacy this little cosmos of the court as do the folios in the *Tacuina*.

Scenes set against a religious background, on the other hand, even if interpreted secularly, always lead to a more realistic portrayal of life (as do the illustrations of romances such as those of *Lancelot* and *Guiron*, to mention two of the most successful examples). Life surges on beyond the palace walls, whereas within the confines of the court everything seems to reach a conclusion in the atmosphere of a happy fable.

THE "TACUINUM" OF ROUEN

Ms. 3054 in the Town Library at Rouen is unquestionably the latest among the *Tacuina* we have been considering.

Professor Wickersheimer was the first to link it to those in Paris, Vienna, and the Casanatense Library—naturally not to that of Liège, which was unknown to him. The comparison of their texts made it possible to note the similarity of the brief introduction in the Rouen codex to that which appears in the Casanatense manuscript. We may add that these introductory lines, even if with some variations, also appear in the Vienna manuscript, whereas those in Liège and Paris contain only a very abbreviated phrase. Wickersheimer pointed out that this brief introduction in the Rouen codex represents almost one-third of Ibn Botlân's entire text as it appears in the printed edition (1531) of the Latin translation. With extreme caution he thus attributed the manuscript to the Italian milieu of the 1400s, on the basis of that humanistic writing of which it is undoubtedly a successful example.

The Rouen *Tacuinum* was part of the great 1958 Milan exhibition of *Lombard Art from the Visconti to the Sforza*. A comparison with the Casanatense manuscript undoubtedly reveals a certain rapport that I subscribe to only in accordance with the terms proposed by Professor Wickersheimer, who observed that, in regard to the illuminations: "They remind us in a striking manner of those in the Casanatense manuscript, even if smaller in dimension." He concludes by formulating the hypothesis that the two manuscripts were derived from a common model.

As far as pinpointing the Italian area in which the Rouen *Tacuinum* was realized in both its writing and decoration, no exact hypothesis has been formulated, and even Renata Cipriani, in the paper prepared for the Milan exhibition, limited herself to pointing out the recognizably humanistic writing, describing the manuscript as a "refined imitation of those *Tacuina* executed at the end of the 1300s," placing this codex at the beginning of the 1400s.

In examining the first folio, which differs noticeably from those in the other manuscripts, I would be tempted to think of a work undertaken by an illuminator of Tuscan background and training. Both the person standing with the book in his hand and the man sitting at his desk tend, by the very simplicity of their clothing (which leans more toward an indication of volume than that descriptive attention to detail so dear to the hearts of the Lombards), to suggest the manner of the Florentine fresco painters who were active during the early 1400s.

The overall impression one receives when leafing through the folios is of a preeminent interest in drawing; all the forms are lightened, in a certain sense schematized, in comparison to the Vienna and Casanatense manuscripts. The notes on the environment are strongly synthesized. Folio 35v is particularly indicative in this sense. To the lively description of the environment found in the Vienna *Tacuinum* (almost symbolic in its emphasis of interest in reality under all of its manifold aspects, which was typical of works done in the Po Valley) is opposed the solitary figure of a girl in this manuscript. The folio in the Casanatense manuscript devoted to the same subject, f. LXXXV, also reveals a greater discursive intent by the presence of two people.

Another folio that would induce us to consider the illuminator to have been of Tuscan formation is that folio (f. 36v) which shows two persons in an enclosed garden, their dishes filled with chicken wings and necks. Two small trees, one certainly a cypress, emerge from over the wall in the manner typical of Florentine painting in the 1400s. One has only to think, for example, of the frescoes by Baldovinetti in San Miniato.

It is interesting to note that the folios in which elements alien to the Po Valley are most evident are those that do not correspond to the Casanatense manuscript. In addition to the previously mentioned f. 35v (rice bread), and f. 36v (chicken wings and necks), f. 26v (escarole) and f. 26 (purslane) do not appear in any of the other *Tacuina* we have considered. Also, in these last two folios the interest in volume and drawing per se is predominant. In the folio for escarole the thickness of the sods upon which the greens sprout is almost palpable. The greens are fanned out symmetrically in a way that has nothing to do with a realistic representation, but rather expresses an intellectualized translation of a first naturalistic suggestion. The two flexible small trees further balance symmetrically that composition whose center is still constituted by the human figure. The woman we might say is busy picking the greens, but whatever precise gesture she may be performing becomes only secondary in a representation that ignores the realistic intention of folios depicting similar topics which we have considered in relation to Manfredus de Monte Imperiali in the *Historia Plantarum* and in the other *Tacuina*. The folio for purslane introduces us to a world framed by a circular enclosure that underlines a geometric conception of space. This aspect also leads us back to Tuscany, since the circumscribed gardens of Verona are quite different. It is sufficient to think of Stefano da Zevio or of those drawings evident in Lombard illuminations of about 1480, or even illustrations produced in the Rhine area.

The question of the attribution of this manuscript to the Po Valley milieu, to Tuscany, or to some other area difficult to pinpoint owing to the constant interchange of artists among the workshops permits us to hypothesize concerning the success of the *Tacuinum* in various milieus. This had already been clearly indicated by other manuscripts—which we have mentioned above—belonging to the German and the Venetian areas.

The small codex in Rouen, undoubtedly of lesser quality than the other *Tacuina* we have considered, offers us images now familiar but still useful, in that it has made it possible to emphasize a moment of illuminated realization of the genre of *Tacuinum Sanitatis* in a vein which had become more Humanistic than Gothic.

ACKNOWLEDGMENTS

The author and the publisher wish to thank the Cassa di Risparmio of the Lombard Provinces, the University Library in Liège, the Town Library in Rouen, the National Library in Paris, the National Library in Vienna, the Casanatense Library in Rome, and the Photographic Archives of the City of Milan for their cooperation in the preparation of this volume.

A heartfelt expression of thanks is also extended by the author to Dr. Mirko Zagnoli, who, with the utmost liberality, allowed me to draw from the now irreplaceable photographic archives of the Cassa di Risparmio; to Professor Hoyoux for the cordial reception he accorded me at the University of Liège, as well as for his valuable suggestions; and to Dr. Carlo Pirovano for the very useful and lively exchanges of ideas on the multiple problems of uncertain resolution posed by a study of this nature.

NOTES TO THE PLATES

The transcriptions of the codices of Liège and Rouen are offered here for the first time, whereas for the other three codices previous transcriptions have been very useful.

We have deemed it advisable to indicate with dots both the impossibility of transcribing words that time has rendered illegible and those cases where we could not arrive at an acceptable interpretation.

The color plates are presented according to an alphabetical arrangement of the Latin names for the various subjects. For the black-and-white plates section, precedence was given to the hitherto unpublished Liège *Tacuinum*, following the numerical progression of the folios, whereas for the other codices the subjects have been grouped according to an alphabetical arrangement of their Latin names. (In the English translations of the commentaries for all plates, the name of the element has been given first in English and then in Latin.)

The Latin transcriptions, the Table of Concordance, and the List of Related Manuscripts have been prepared by Dr. Marina Righetti.

(For the complete philological and critical documentation, and further iconographic references, see the original Italian edition.)

COLOR PLATES

I. DILL (*ANETI*)

Nature: Warm and dry toward the end of the second degree and the beginning of the third. *Optimum:* The kind that is green, fresh, and tender. *Usefulness:* Brings relief to a stomach that is cold and windy. *Dangers:* It is harmful to the kidneys and causes nausea with its essence. *Neutralization of the Dangers:* With *lemoncellis* (juice of small lemons?). *Effects:* Moderately nourishing. It is good for cold and damp temperaments, for old people, in Winter and in cold regions. (*Vienna,* f. 32)

II. WARM WATER (*AQUA CALIDA*)

Nature: Cold and humid in the second degree. *Optimum:* Lukewarm and sweet. *Usefulness:* It cleans the stomach lining. *Dangers:* It weakens the mechanism of digestion. *Neutralization of the Dangers:* By mixing with rose water. *Effects:* Can cause moist swellings. It is primarily recommended for cold temperaments, for old people, in Winter, and in cold regions. (*Vienna*, f. 89)

III. AUTUMN (*AUTUMPNUS*)

Nature: Moderately cold in the second degree. *Optimum:* Its central period. *Usefulness:* When one proceeds gradually toward opposites, as for example, toward warmth and dampness. *Dangers:* It is harmful to moderate temperaments and to those predisposed toward consumption. *Neutralization of the Dangers:* By the application of moist elements, and with baths. *Effects:* Increases melancholy humors. It is suitable to warm and damp temperaments, to the young and adolescent, in warm and damp regions, or in temperate areas. (*Vienna,* f. 54v)

IV. BEETS (*BLETE*)

Nature: Warm and dry in the first degree. *Optimum:* Those with a sweet taste. *Usefulness:* Their juice eliminates dandruff. *Dangers:* They set the blood on fire. *Neutralization of the Dangers:* With vinegar and mustard. (*Rouen,* f. 24v)

V. CHESTNUTS (*CASTANEE*)

Nature: Warm in the first degree, dry in the second.
Optimum: The marrons of Brianza, well ripened.
Usefulness: They exercise an influence over coitus
and are very nourishing. *Dangers:* They inflate, and
cause headaches. *Neutralization of the Dangers:*
Cooking them in water. (*Rouen,* f. 31)

VI. CABBAGE (*CAULES ONATI*)

Nature: Warm in the first degree, dry in the second.
Optimum: The fresh and fleshy ones. *Usefulness:*
They remove obstructions. *Dangers:* They are bad
for the intestines. *Neutralization of the Dangers:*
With much oil. (*Rouen*, f. 20)

VII. SOUR CHERRIES (*CERESA ACETOSA*)

Nature: Cold at the end of the first degree, humid in the first. *Optimum:* The pulpy ones with a thin skin. *Usefulness:* Good for phlegmatic stomachs burdened with superfluities. *Dangers:* They are digested slowly. *Neutralization of the Dangers:* By eating them on an empty stomach. (*Casanatense,* f. XVII)

VIII. ORANGES (*CETRONA ID EST NARANCIA*)

Nature: The pulp is cold and humid in the third degree, the skin is dry and warm in the second. *Optimum:* Those that are perfectly ripe. *Usefulness:* Their candied skin is good for the stomach. *Dangers:* They are difficult to digest. *Neutralization of the Dangers:* Accompanied by the best wine. (*Rouen,* f. 34v)

IX. COITUS (*COYTUS*)

Nature: It is the union of two for the purpose of introducing the sperm. *Optimum:* That which lasts until the sperm has been completely emitted. *Usefulness:* It preserves the species. *Dangers:* It is harmful to those with cold and dry breathing. *Neutralization of the Dangers:* With sperm-producing foods. (*Paris,* f. 100v)

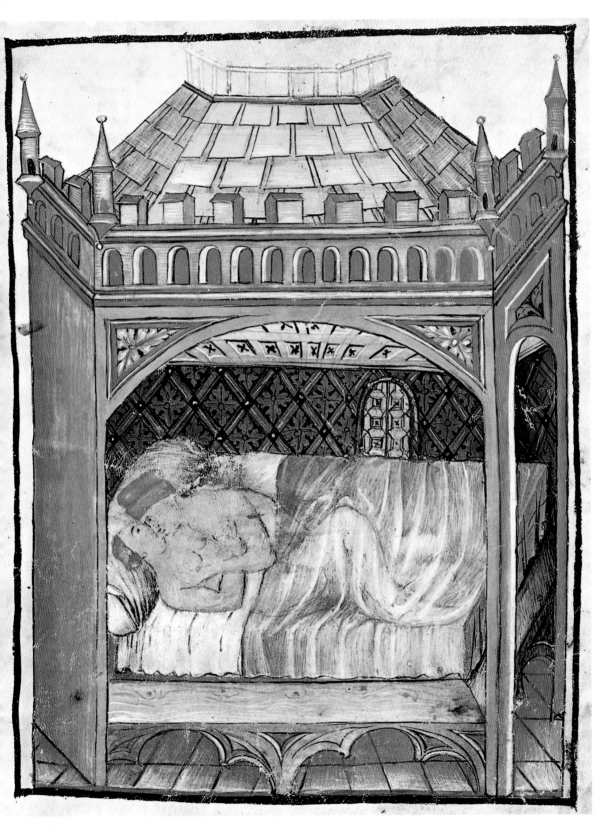

Cuammeris
z certili.

XI. SQUASH (*CUCURBITE*)

Nature: Cold and humid in the second degree. *Optimum:* Those that are fresh and green. *Usefulness:* They quench thirst. *Dangers:* They constitute a swift laxative. *Neutralization of the Dangers:* With salted water and mustard. *Effects:* A moderate and cold nourishment. They are good for choleric temperaments, for the young, in Summer, in all regions, and above all in Southern areas. (*Vienna*, f. 22v)

X. WATERMELONS AND CUCUMBERS (*CUCUMERES ET CETRULI*)

Nature: (According to Johannes), cold and humid in the second degree. *Optimum:* Those that are large and full. *Usefulness:* They cool hot fevers and purify the urine. *Dangers:* . . . they cause pain in the loins and in the stomach. *Neutralization of the Dangers:* With honey and oil. (*Paris,* f. 38v)

XII. SUMMER (*ESTAS*)

Nature: Warm in the third degree, dry in the second,
Optimum: For the body—its beginning. *Usefulness:*
It overcomes superfluities and cold diseases. *Dangers:*
It slows down digestion and increases bilious humors. *Neutralization of the Dangers:* With a humid
diet in a cool environment. *Effects:* Increases bilious
humors and dry substances. It is good for cold temperaments, for old people, and in Northern regions.
(*Vienna*, f. 54)

XIII. FENNEL (*FENICULUS*)

Nature: Warm and dry in the second degree. *Optimum:* The domestic variety. *Usefulness:* Good for the eyesight and for prolonged fevers. *Dangers:* It is bad for the menstrual flow. *Neutralization of the Dangers:* With . . . of carob. (*Casanatense,* f. LXXVI)

XIV. WHEAT (*FURMENTUM*)

Nature: Warm and humid in the second degree.
Optimum: Plump and heavy grains. *Usefulness:*
Opens abscesses. *Dangers:* Causes obstructions. *Neu-tralization of the Dangers:* When it is well prepared.
(*Casanatense*, F. LXXVIII)

XV. ACORNS (*GLANDES*)

Nature: Cold in the second degree, dry in the third.
Optimum: Those that are fresh and large. *Useful-*
ness: They help retention. *Dangers:* They prevent
menstruation. *Neutralization of the Dangers:* By eating them roasted and with sugar. (*Rouen*, f. 29)

XVI. SOUR POMEGRANATES
(*GRANATA ACETOSA*)

Nature: Cold in the second degree and humid in the
first. *Optimum:* Those that are very watery. *Usefulness:* Good for a warm liver. *Dangers:* Bad for the
chest and the voice. *Neutralization of the Dangers:*
With honeyed foods. (*Rouen*, f. 4v)

XVII. WINTER (*HYEMPS*)

Nature: Cold in the third degree, humid in the second, when it is normal. *Optimum:* Its final period. *Usefulness:* Good for diseases of the liver and helpful to the digestion. *Dangers:* It is harmful to phlegmatic diseases and increases phlegm. *Neutralization of the Dangers:* With fire and heavy clothing. It is good for warm and dry temperaments, for the young, in Southern regions and in those close to the sea. (*Vienna*, f. 55)

XVIII. LETTUCE (*LACTUCE*)

Nature: Cold and humid in the second degree. *Optimum:* Those with large leaves and of a lemon-yellow color. *Usefulness:* Relieves insomnia and spermatorrhea. *Dangers:* It is harmful to coitus and to the eyesight. *Neutralization of the Dangers:* By mixing it with celery. (*Rouen,* f. 10)

XIX. SWEET MARJORAM (*MAIORANA*)

Nature: Warm and dry in the third degree. *Optimum:* The very small and aromatic variety. *Usefulness:* It is good for a cold and humid stomach. *Dangers:* None. *Effects:* It purifies the blood. It is good for cold and humid temperaments, for old people, in Winter, in Autumn, and in cold regions. (*Vienna*, f. 33v)

XX. THE FRUIT OF THE MANDRAGORA
(FRUCTUS MANDRAGORE)

Nature: Cold in the third degree, dry in the second.
Optimum: The highly fragrant variety. *Usefulness:* √
Smelling it helps alleviate headaches and insomnia;
spreading it on the skin works against elephantiasis
and black infections. *Dangers:* It stupefies the senses.
Neutralization of the Dangers: With the fruits of ivy.
Effects: It is not comestible. It is good for warm
temperaments, for the young, in Summer, and in the
Southern regions. (*Vienna*, f. 40)

XXI. INDUS OR PALESTINIAN MELONS
(*MELONES INDI IDEST PALESTINI*)

Nature: Cold and humid in the second degree. *Optimum:* Those that are sweet and watery. *Usefulness:* Good in illnesses. *Dangers:* Bad for the digestion. *Neutralization of the Dangers:* With barley-sugar. (*Rouen*, f. 19)

anlium.

XXII. MILLET (*MILIUM*)

Nature: Cold and dry in the second degree. *Optimum:* That which is left in the field for three months. *Usefulness:* Good for those who wish to refresh the✓ stomach and dry out superfluous humors. *Dangers:* Not very nourishing. *Neutralization of the Dangers:* Consumed together with nourishing foods. (*Paris,* f. 52v)

XXIII. TURNIPS (*NAPONES*)

Nature: Warm in the second degree, humid in the first. *Optimum:* Those that are long and dark. *Usefulness:* They increase sperm and make the body less subject to swellings. *Dangers:* They cause occlusions of the veins. *Neutralization of the Dangers:* Stewed twice and consumed with very fat meats. (*Paris,* f. 43)

XXIV. OIL OF ALMONDS (*OLEUM AMIGDOLARUM*)

Nature: Moderately warm in the second degree, humid in the first. *Optimum:* The fresh and sweet variety. *Usefulness:* Good for the stomach, the chest, and for a cough. *Dangers:* Bad for weak intestines. *Neutralization of the Dangers:* With mastic. *Effects:* Generates moderate humors. It is particularly recommended for temperate bodies, for adolescents, in Spring, and in the Eastern regions. (*Vienna,* f. 91)

XXV. OLIVE OIL (*OLEUM OLIUE*)

Nature: (According to Albulcasem), warm and humid. *Optimum:* . . . good month. *Usefulness:* It fattens and is easily digestible. *Dangers:* It puts the stomach to sleep and is transformed. *Neutralization of the Dangers:* Mixed with foods. (*Paris,* f. 15)

XXVI. PARTRIDGES (*PERDICES*)

Nature: Of moderate warmth. *Optimum:* Those that are moist and fat. *Usefulness:* Good for convalescing people. *Dangers:* Bad for those engaged in heavy labor. *Neutralization of the Dangers:* Cooking them with leavened dough. (*Casanatense, f.* CXXVIII)

XXVII. PINE CONES (*PINEE*)

Nature: Warm in the second degree, dry in the first. *Optimum:* . . . *Usefulness:* They stimulate the bladder, the kidneys, and the libido. *Dangers:* Worms hatch in their bark. *Neutralization of the Dangers:* Trim the tree often. (*Paris,* f. 14)

Pinee. barou· ſſſſ̃·

XXVIII. LEEKS (*PORI*)

Nature: Warm in the third degree, dry in the second. *Optimum:* The kind called *naptici,* that is, from the mountains and with a sharp odor. *Usefulness:* They stimulate urination, influence coitus and, mixed with honey, clear up catarrh of the chest. *Dangers:* Bad for the brain and the senses. *Neutralization of the Dangers:* With sesame oil and with the oil of sweet almonds. *Effects:* They cause hot blood and an acute crisis of the bile. They are primarily indicated for cold temperaments, for old people, in Winter, and in the Northerly regions. (*Vienna,* f. 25)

XXIX. *SAVICH* OR BARLEY SOUP
(*SAUICH, ID EST PULTES ORDEI*)

Nature: Cold and dry in the second degree, temperate when it is toasted. *Usefulness:* Promotes the flow of bile. *Dangers:* It generates flatulence. *Neutralization of the Dangers:* With sugar. *Effects:* Encourages positive humors. It is good for hot temperaments, for the young, in Summer, and in the warm regions. (*Vienna,* f. 44v)

XXX. *SAVICH* OR WHEAT SOUP
(*SAUICH, ID EST PULTES TRITICI*)

Nature: Warm and dry in the second degree. *Optimum:* Cooked over moderate heat. *Usefulness:* Good for humid intestines. *Dangers:* It irritates the respiratory passages. *Neutralization of the Dangers:* By mixing it with warm water. *Effects:* It causes the blood to be moderately warm. It is good for moderate temperaments, for old people, in Winter and Spring, and in all regions. (*Vienna,* f. 43v)

XXXI. RICOTTA (*RECOCTA*)

Nature: Cold and humid. *Optimum:* That obtained from pure milk. *Usefulness:* It nourishes the body and fattens it. *Dangers:* It causes occlusions, is difficult to digest, and favors colic. (*Paris,* f. 59)

Recorta.

Rofe.

XXXII. ROSES (*ROXE*)

Nature: (According to Johannes), cold in the first
degree, dry in the third. *Optimum:* The fresh ones
from Suri and Persia. *Usefulness:* Good for inflamed
brains. *Dangers:* They can cause headaches in certain people. *Neutralization of the Dangers:* With
camphor. (*Paris,* f. 83)

XXXIII. ROSES (*ROXE*)

Nature: Cold in the first degree, dry in the third
(others in the second). *Optimum:* The fresh ones
from Suri and Persia. *Usefulness:* Good for inflamed
brains. *Dangers:* In some persons they cause a feeling of heaviness and constriction, or blockage of the
sense of smell. *Neutralization of the Dangers:* With
camphor, at other times with the crocus. *Effects:*
They are good for warm temperaments, for the
young, in warm seasons, and in warm regions.
(*Vienna,* f. 38)

XXXIV. ROSES (*ROXE*)

Nature: Cold in the second degree, dry in the third, *Optimum:* Those from Suri and Persia. *Usefulness:* Good for inflamed brains. *Dangers:* In some persons they cause headaches. *Neutralization of the Dangers:* With camphor. (*Casanatense*, f. LXIX)

XXXV. RUE (*RUTA*)

Nature: Warm and dry in the third degree. *Optimum:* That which is grown near a fig tree. *Usefulness:* It sharpens the eyesight and dissipates flatulence. *Dangers:* It augments the sperm and dampens the desire for coitus. *Neutralization of the Dangers:* With foods that multiply the sperm. (*Paris,* f. 32)

Ruta.

XXXVI. SAGE (*SALUIA*)

Nature: Warm in the first degree and dry in the second. *Optimum:* The domestic kind and, above all, its leaves. *Usefulness:* It is good for paralysis and for the nerves. *Dangers:* It removes the dark color from the hair. *Neutralization of the Dangers:* With a potion in which there is myrtle and garden crocus. (*Casanatense,* f. LXVIII)

XXXVII. RYE (*SILIGO*)

Nature: Cold and dry in the second degree. *Optimum:* That which has been thoroughly ripened. *Usefulness:* It breaks down the concentration of humors. *Dangers:* Bad for those suffering from colic or melancholia. *Neutralization of the Dangers:* With plenty of wheat. (*Casanatense*, f. LXXXVI)

Sparagus

XXXVIII. ASPARAGUS (*SPARAGUS*)

Nature: (According to Johannes), its nature is moderately warm and moist in the first degree. *Optimum:* The fresh kind whose tip is turned downward toward the earth. *Usefulness:* It influences coitus positively and removes occlusions. *Dangers:* It is bad for the stomach lining. *Neutralization of the Dangers:* Boiled and then seasoned with salted water. (*Paris,* f. 26)

XXXIX. SPELT (*SPELTA*)

Nature: Warm quality. *Optimum:* The heaviest and most ponderous. *Usefulness:* Good for the chest, for the lungs, and for a cough. *Dangers:* It is harmful to the stomach and is less nourishing than wheat. *Neutralization of the Dangers:* By consuming it with anise. (*Casanatense,* f. LXXXVII)

XL. SPINACH (*SPINACHIE*)

Nature: Cold and humid in the first degree, of moderate warmth at other times. *Optimum:* Those leaves still wet with rain water. *Usefulness:* They are good — for a cough and for the chest. *Dangers:* They disturb the digestion. *Neutralization of the Dangers:* Fried with salted water, or with vinegar and aromatic herbs. *Effects:* Moderately nourishing. They are good for warm temperaments, for the young, at all times, and in every region. (*Vienna*, f. 27)

XLI. THERIAC (*TRIACHA*)

Nature: Warm and dry. *Optimum:* The kind that
frees the rooster from poison and has been aged for
ten years. *Usefulness:* Good against poisons and both
cold and warm illnesses. *Dangers:* When it is over ten
years old it causes insomnia. *Neutralization of the
Dangers:* With cooling substances such as barley-
water. It is primarily good for cold temperaments,
for old people, in Winter, in cold regions and, if
necessary, anywhere else. (*Vienna,* f. 53v)

XLII. PASTA (*TRIJ*)

Nature: Warm and moist in the second degree. *Optimum:* That which is prepared with great care. *Usefulness:* It is good for the chest and for the throat. ✓ *Dangers:* It is harmful to weak intestines and to the stomach. *Neutralization of the Dangers:* With sweet barley. *Effects:* Very nourishing. It is good for a hot stomach, for the young, in Winter, and in all regions. (*Vienna*, f. 45v)

XLIII. GRAPES (*UVE*)

Nature: Warm in the first degree, moist in the second. *Optimum:* The kind with a thin skin, watery, which protects against poisons. *Usefulness:* They are nourishing, they purify the system, and they fatten. *Dangers:* They cause thirst. *Neutralization of the Dangers:* With sour pomegranates. (*Casanatense*, f. III)

lent' meridionalis.

XLIV. SOUTHERLY WIND (*VENTUS MERIDIONALIS*)

Nature: Warm in the second degree, dry in the first. *Optimum:* The kind that sweeps across favorable regions. *Usefulness:* Good for the chest. *Dangers:* Weakens the senses. *Neutralization of the Dangers:* With baths. (*Paris,* f. 101v)

Ⱳⱳ.

XLV. SPRING (VER)

Nature: Moderate humidity in the second degree.
Optimum: Its central period. *Usefulness:* Good for
all animals and for the products that germinate from
the earth. *Dangers:* Bad for unclean bodies. *Neutralization of the Dangers:* By cleaning the body. (*Paris,*
f. 103)

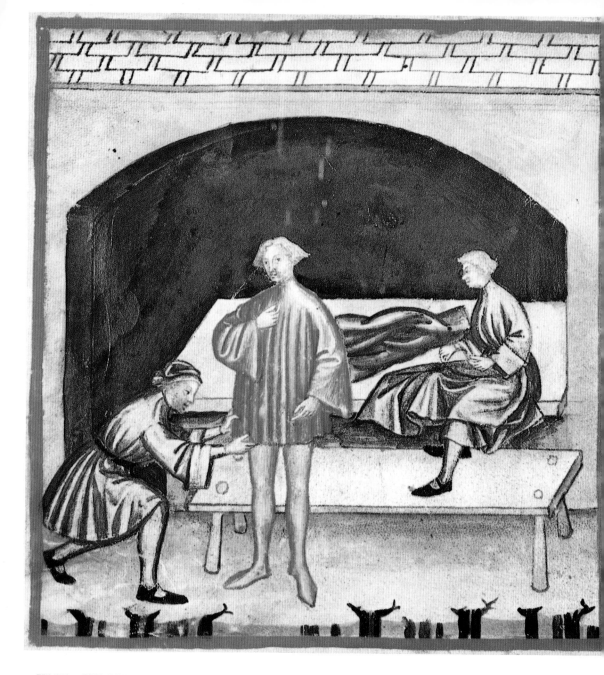

XLVI. WOOLEN CLOTHING (*VESTIS LANEA*)

Nature: Warm and dry. *Optimum:* The thin kind from Flanders. *Usefulness:* It protects the body from cold and holds warmth. *Dangers:* It causes skin irritation. *Neutralization of the Dangers:* With thin linen clothing. (*Casanatense*, f. CCVI)

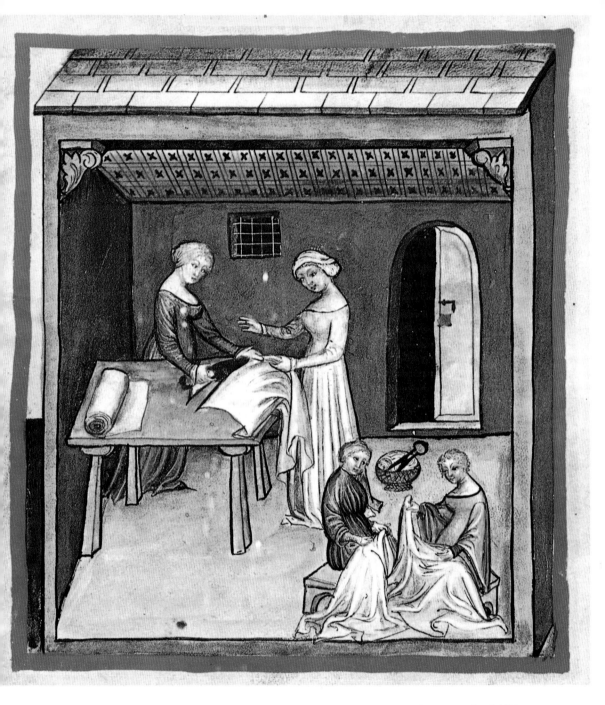

XLVII. LINEN CLOTHING (*VESTIS LINEA*)

Nature: Cold and dry in the second degree. *Optimum:* The light, splendid, beautiful kind. *Usefulness:* It moderates the heat of the body. *Dangers:* It presses down on the skin and blocks transpiration. *Neutralization of the Dangers:* By mixing it with silk. *Effects:* It dries up ulcerations. It is primarily good for hot temperaments, for the young, in Summer, and in the Southern regions. (*Vienna*, f. 105v)

XLVIII. SUGAR (*CUCHARUM*)

Nature: Warm in the first degree, humid in the second. *Optimum:* The white, clear kind. *Usefulness:* It purifies the body, is good for the chest, the kidneys, and the bladder. *Dangers:* It causes thirst and moves bilious humors. *Neutralization of the Dangers:* With sour pomegranates. *Effects:* Produces blood that is not bad. It is good for all temperaments, at all ages, in every season and region. (*Vienna*, f. 92)

BLACK AND WHITE PLATES
AND DOCUMENTATION

A. THE TACUINUM OF LIEGE

1. ALBULLASEM DE BALDAC, SON OF HABDI THE PHYSICIAN, COMPOSED THIS BOOK.

Hereafter are named all the men of wisdom who have a place in this book, and they are indicated by means of an initial from their names.

Ypo. with a Greek Y, Ga. by G, Ru. by Ru, Dya. by D, Pa. by P, Ou. by O, Teo. by T, Jo. by Jo, Ma. by Ma, Ve. by ve, Schi by schi, Ra. by ra, Mu. by mu, Jo by a Latin J, Jsa. by is, Albu. by al.

Keep in mind that medicine speaks of four degrees, that is, 1st, 2nd, 3rd, 4th, and no more.

(f. 1v)

2. FIGS (FICHUS)

Nature: Warm and humid in the first degree. *Optimum:* Those that are white and peeled. *Usefulness:* They purify the kidneys and clean them of gravel. *Dangers:* They inflate and thicken. *Neutralization of the Dangers:* With salted water and sour syrup.

(f. 2)

3. GRAPES (UVE)

Nature: Humid here. *Optimum:* The large kind, with a thin skin and watery. *Usefulness:* They nourish, purge, and fatten. *Dangers:* They cause thirst. *Neutralization of the Dangers:* With sour pomegranates.

(f. 2v)

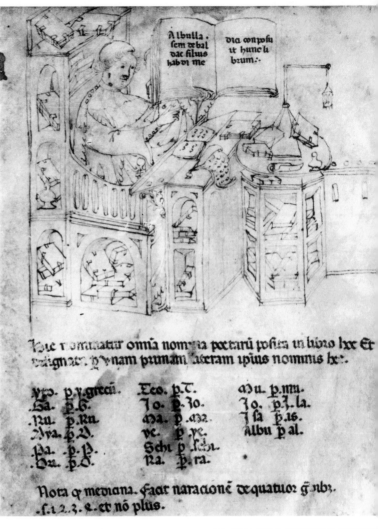

PEACHES (PERSICHA)

Nature: Cold and humid in the first degree. *Optimum:* Those called muscat. *Usefulness:* Against hot fevers. *Dangers:* They break down humors. *Neutralization of the Dangers:* With fragrant wine. (f. 3)

PLUMS (BRUGNA)

Nature: Cold in the second degree. *Optimum:* The sweet kind, called *calaone*. *Usefulness:* They purify bilious humors. *Dangers:* They harm the stomach lining. *Neutralization of the Dangers:* With rose-colored sugar. (f. 3v)

6. PEARS (PIRA)

Nature: Cold in the first degree, dry in the second. *Optimum:* Those ripened the natural way. *Usefulness:* For weak stomachs. *Dangers:* Colic. *Neutralization of the Dangers:* Eating other things after them. (f. 4)

7. SWEET POMEGRANATES (GRANATA DULCIA)

Nature: Warm in the first degree, humid in the second. *Optimum:* Those which are . . . and large. *Usefulness:* Good for a cough and for coitus. *Dangers:* They produce swellings. *Neutralization of the Dangers:* With sour pomegranates. (f. 4v)

8. SOUR POMEGRANATES (GRANATA ACCETOSA)

Nature: Cold in the second degree, humid in the first. *Optimum:* Those that are very watery. *Usefulness:* Good for a hot liver. *Dangers:* Bad for the chest and the voice. *Neutralization of the Dangers:* With foods and honey. (f. 5)

9. QUINCE (CITONIA COLONIA)

Nature: Cold and dry in the second degree. *Optimum:* Those which are large and full. *Usefulness:* They cheer people up and stimulate them. *Dangers:* Bad for colic. *Neutralization of the Dangers:* With dates and honey. (f. 5v)

10. SWEET APPLES (POMA MALA DULCIA)

Nature: Warm and humid in the second degree. *Optimum:* Those called *para-dixani* and *gerosolimitani*. *Usefulness:* They comfort the heart. *Dangers:* To the nerves. *Neutralization of the Dangers:* With rose-colored sugar or rose-colored honey.
(f. 6)

11. SOUR APPLES (POMA MALA ACCETOSA)

Nature: Cold and dry in the second degree. *Optimum:* Those that do not come from Pontus. *Usefulness:* For fainting. *Dangers:* To the joints. *Neutralization of the Dangers:* With fragrant, yellow-colored wine.
(f. 6v)

12. APRICOTS (ARMONIACA)

Nature: Cold and humid in the second degree. *Optimum:* Those *armui* (from Armenia?) and *barni*. *Usefulness:* They induce vomiting. *Dangers:* They cool the stomach greatly. *Neutralization of the Dangers:* By vomiting.
(f. 7)

13. SYCAMORE (. . . SICOMORI)

Nature: Cold and humid in the second degree. *Optimum:* Those that are large and black. *Usefulness:* For ulcerations of the throat. *Dangers:* They cause stomach aches. *Neutralization of the Dangers:* With mild medications.
(f. 7v)

14. MEDLAR (NESPULA)

Nature: Cold in the first degree, dry i the second. *Optimum:* .... *Usefulnes* They protect against drunkenness. *Da gers:* To the stomach and to digestio *Neutralization of the Dangers:* Wi barley-sugar.
(f. 8)

15. MORELLO CHERRIES (CEREXA ACETOXE)

Nature: Cold and humid in the first de gree. *Optimum:* The sweet ones with thin skin. *Usefulness:* To a phlegmati stomach full of superfluities. *Danger* They are digested slowly. *Neutraliza tion:* By eating them on an empty stom ach.
(f. 8v)

6. SWEET CHERRIES (CEREXA DULCIA)

Nature: Cold and humid in the first degree. *Optimum:* The ripe and sweet ones. *Usefulness:* They display moistening properties and soften the abdomen. *Dangers:* To the stomach, if abused. *Neutralization of the Dangers:* With yellow-colored wine.
(f. 9)

7. SWEET ALMONDS (AMIGDALE DULCES)

Nature: Warm and dry in the second degree. *Optimum:* Those whose skin flakes off when rubbed. *Usefulness:* They delay drunkenness. *Dangers:* They irritate. *Neutralization of the Dangers:* By drinking the best wine and yellow-colored wine.
(f. 9v)

18. GARDEN NASTURTIUMS (RUCOLA MASTURCIUM)

Nature: Warm and humid in the first degree. *Optimum:* The kind that are less strong in flavor. *Usefulness:* They increase coitus and sperm. *Dangers:* They cause headaches. *Neutralization of the Dangers:* With endive salad, lettuce, and vinegar.
(f. 10)

19. SAGE (SALUIA)

Nature: Warm in the first degree, dry in the second. *Optimum:* The domestic variety. *Usefulness:* For paralysis and the nerves. *Dangers:* Removes the dark color from the hair. *Neutralization of the Dangers:* With a rinse in which there is some myrtle and oriental crocus.
(f. 16)

20. SQUASH (CUCURBITE)

Nature: Cold and humid in the second degree. *Optimum:* Those that are fresh and green. *Usefulness:* They quench thirst. *Dangers:* They change and are absorbed too quickly. *Neutralization of the Dangers:* With salted water and mustard.
(f. 18v)

21. TRUFFLES (TARTUFULLUS)

Nature: Cold and humid in the second degree. *Optimum:* The large ones shaped like an eggplant. *Usefulness:* They absorb all flavors and influence coitus positively. *Dangers:* For melancholy diseases. *Neutralization of the Dangers:* With pepper, oil, and honey.
(f. 41v)

22. FENNEL (FENICULUS)

Nature: Warm and dry in the second degree. *Optimum:* The domestic variety. *Usefulness:* For the eyesight and for fevers of long duration. *Dangers:* A negative effect on the menstrual flow. *Neutralization of the Dangers:* With *troxicis derabe.*
(f. 24v)

23. TURNIPS (NAPONES)

Nature: Warm in the second degree and humid in the first. *Optimum:* The long and dark ones. *Usefulness:* They increase the sperm and render the flesh less prone to swellings. *Dangers:* Occlusions in the veins and the pores. *Neutralization of the Dangers:* Stewed twice and served with very fat meats.
(f. 24)

24. BEANS (FAXOLLI)

Nature: Warm and humid in the first degree. *Optimum:* The red, whole ones. *Usefulness:* They stimulate urination and fatten. *Dangers:* They make . . . *Neutralization of the Dangers:* With oil, salted water, and mustard.
(f. 26)

25. CHICK PEA SOUP (BRONDIUM CEXERUM)

Nature: Warm and humid in the second degree. *Optimum:* That which is prepared with chick peas, broad beans, and sweet milk. *Usefulness:* For paralysis. *Dangers:* For bilious humors. *Neutralization of the Dangers:* With *stibeis.*
(f. 27v)

26. WHEAT (FURMENTUM)

Nature: Warm and humid in the seco degree. *Optimum:* The large and hea grains. *Usefulness:* It opens ulceratio *Dangers:* It causes occlusions. *Neutr ization of the Dangers:* By thorou cooking.
(f. 28)

27. RYE (SILLIGO)

Nature: Cold and dry. *Optimum:* Th which is full and well matured. *Usef ness:* Breaks down the concentration humors. *Dangers:* For those sufferi from colic or from melancholy. *Neutr ization of the Dangers:* With go wheat.
(f. 28v)

  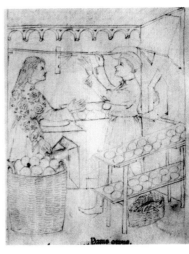

28. MILLET (MILLIUM)

Nature: Cold in the first, dry in the second degree. *Optimum:* That which has been ripened in the field for at least three months. *Usefulness:* For those who need to refresh their stomachs and to dry up humors. *Dangers:* Not very nourishing. *Neutralization of the Dangers:* By consuming it with highly nourishing foods.
(f. 31)

29. WHEAT SOUP (PULCES FURMENTI)

Nature: Cold and humid in the second degree. *Optimum:* Cooked over moderate heat. *Usefulness:* For humid intestines. *Dangers:* It irritates the respiratory tract. *Neutralization of the Dangers:* By washing the grains with warm water.
(f. 33)

30. BOILED WHEAT (FURMENTUM ELIXUM)

Nature: Cold and humid in the second degree. *Optimum:* That which is large and thoroughly baked. *Usefulness:* For bodies that abound in salts. *Dangers:* Generates flatulence and many superfluities. *Neutralization of the Dangers:* With much salt.
(f. 33v)

31. BARLEY SOUP (PULTES ORDEI)

Nature: Cold and dry in the second degree. *Optimum:* That which has been cooked over moderate heat. *Usefulness:* Facilitates the flowing of bilious humors. *Dangers:* Generates swellings. *Neutralization of the Dangers:* With sugar.
(f. 34)

32. VERY FINE WHITE BREAD (PANIS DE SIMILA ALBISSIMUS)

Nature: . . . and warm in the second degree. *Optimum:* That which is well baked and yellow-colored. *Usefulness:* It fattens the body. *Dangers:* It causes occlusions. *Neutralization of the Dangers:* Through its complete leavening.
(f. 34v)

33. BLACK BREAD (PANIS OPPUS)

Nature: Warm in the second degree. *Optimum:* The kind with less bran, left overnight after baking before eating. *Usefulness:* It soothes the intestines. *Dangers:* It causes itching and scabies. *Neutralization of the Dangers:* With . . .
(f. 35)

34. UNLEAVENED BREAD (PANIS AZIMUS)

Nature: Warm and dry, moderately cold in the second degree. *Optimum:* That which is salted and baked very well. *Usefulness:* For bodies abounding in salts. *Dangers:* Generates swellings. *Neutralization of the Dangers:* With old wine.
(f. 35v)

35. SWEET MILK (LAC DULCE)

Nature: Temperate and sweet when warm. *Optimum:* That from young sheep. *Usefulness:* For the chest and lungs. *Dangers:* for fevers. *Neutralization of the Dangers:* With seedless raisins.
(f. 37v)

36. BUTTER (BUTIRUM)

Nature: Warm and moist. *Optimum:* That which is made from sheep's milk. *Usefulness:* Against superfluities in the lungs caused by the cold or by dryness. *Dangers:* Renders the stomach apathetic. *Neutralization of the Dangers:* With astringent substances.
(f. 39)

37. FRESH CHEESE (CASEUS RECENS)

Nature: Warm and moist. *Optimum:* That which is made from the milk of healthy animals. *Usefulness:* Softens the body and fattens it. *Dangers:* Causes occlusions. *Neutralization of the Dangers:* With walnuts, almonds, and with honey.
(f. 39v)

38. OLD CHEESE (CASSEUS VETUS)

Nature: Dry and of moderate warmth. *Optimum:* That which is rich in fats. *Usefulness:* Roasted, it placates dysentery. *Dangers:* For the kidneys and the formation of stones. *Neutralization of the Dangers:* By eating it between two other servings.
(f. 40)

39. RICOTTA (RECOCTA)

Nature: Cold and moist. *Optimum:* That which is made from pure milk. *Usefulness:* It nourishes and fattens. *Dangers:* It causes occlusions in the stomach, is difficult to digest, and is conducive to colic. *Neutralization of the Dangers:* With butter and honey.
(f. 40v)

40. CHICKEN EGGS (OUA GALINEARUM)

Nature: The albumen is cold and moist, the yolk is warm and moist. *Optimum:* Those which are fresh and large. *Usefulness:* They increase coitus noticeably. *Dangers:* They slow down digestion and cause freckles. *Neutralization of the Dangers:* By eating only the yolk. (f. 41v)

41. OSTRICH EGGS (OUA AUSTRUM ET GROSSA)

Nature: Large and temperate as to warmth. *Optimum:* .... *Usefulness:* For those involved in strenuous activities. *Dangers:* For colic; they also cause flatulence and vertigo. *Neutralization of the Dangers:* With oregano and salt. (f. 42)

42. RAM MEAT (CARNES ARIETUM)

Nature: Warm and humid in the first degree. *Optimum:* That which has been fattened during the course of a year. *Usefulness:* For the temperate stomach. *Dangers:* For those who suffer habitually from nausea. *Neutralization of the Dangers:* With astringent broths. (f. 42v)

43. KID MEAT (CARNES EDORUM)

Nature: Of moderate warmth in the second degree. *Optimum:* That which is red, tending toward brown. *Usefulness:* It is quickly digested. *Dangers:* For colic (when the meat is roasted). *Neutralization of the Dangers:* ... (f. 43)

44. CALF MEAT (CARNES VITULORUM)

Nature: Of temperate warmth in the second degree. *Optimum:* That which comes from newly born animals. *Usefulness:* For those engaged in heavy work. *Dangers:* For those affected with disorders of the spleen. *Neutralization of the Dangers:* With exercise and baths. (f. 43v)

45. COW MEAT AND CAMEL MEAT (CARNES VACINE ET CAMELORUM)

Nature: Warm and dry in the second degree. *Optimum:* That which comes from young and active animals. *Usefulness:* For those engaged in heavy work and those suffering from bilious disorders. *Dangers:* For those who suffer from melancholia. *Neutralization of the Dangers:* With ginger and pepper. (f. 44)

46. PORK (CARNES PORCINE)

Nature: Warm and humid in the first degree. *Optimum:* That which comes from young and fat animals. *Usefulness:* It is very nourishing and quickly transformed. *Dangers:* Bothers the stomach. *Neutralization of the Dangers:* Roasted and then seasoned with mustard. (f. 44v)

47. MEAT OF GELDED ANIMALS (ANIMALIA CASTRATA)

Nature: Superior to and colder than the meat of nongelded animals. *Optimum:* That which comes from one or two-year-old animals. *Usefulness:* It is quickly digestible. *Dangers:* Laxative for the stomach. *Neutralization of the Dangers:* With fruit juices. (f. 45)

48. GAZELLE MEAT (CARNES CAZELLARUM)

Nature: Warm and dry in the second degree. *Optimum:* That which comes from smaller animals. *Usefulness:* For colic and paralysis. *Dangers:* Desiccates the nerves. *Neutralization of the Dangers:* With oil and vinegar. (f. 45v)

49. HARE MEAT (CARNES LEPORINE)

Nature: Warm and dry in the second degree. *Optimum:* That obtained from animals captured by hunting dogs. *Usefulness:* For those suffering from obesity. *Dangers:* Causes insomnia. *Neutralization of the Dangers:* With spices of subtle substance. (f. 46)

50. TRIPE (BUSECA)

Nature: Cold and dry in the second degree. *Optimum:* That which comes from a ram. *Usefulness:* For those whose food ferments in their stomachs. *Dangers:* To varicosities. *Neutralization of the Dangers:* With ginger and lots of pepper. (f. 48v)

51. CRANE (GRUES)

Nature: Warm and dry in the second degree. *Optimum:* Those captured by falcons. *Usefulness:* For those engaged in heavy work. *Dangers:* They are digested poorly. *Neutralization of the Dangers:* By cooking them with warm spices. (f. 52)

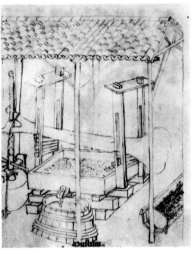

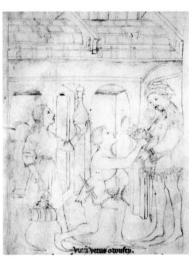

52. QUAIL (QUALIE)

Nature: Warm and moist. *Optimum:* Those which are young and fat. *Usefulness:* For those with an enfeebled aspect. *Dangers:* They cause disturbances. *Neutralization of the Dangers:* With pomegranate wine.
(f. 53v)

53. PEACOCKS (PAUONES)

Nature: Warm and dry in the second degree. *Optimum:* . . . and the youngest among them. *Usefulness:* For warm stomachs. *Dangers:* They are difficult to digest. *Neutralization of the Dangers:* Hanging them with weights.
(f. 54v)

54. GRAPE JUICE (AGRESTA)

Nature: Cold in the third degree, dry in the second. *Optimum:* That which is fresh and clear. *Usefulness:* For intestines suffering from bilious disorders. *Dangers:* For the chest and the nerves. *Neutralization of the Dangers:* With sweet and fat substances.
(f. 56)

55. MUST (MUSTUM)

Nature: Warm and humid in the second degree. *Optimum:* Just pressed. *Usefulness:* Fattens the body. *Dangers:* Generates flatulence. *Neutralization of the Dangers:* With wine from sour pomegranates and with fennel.
(f. 56v)

56. WINE (VINUM)

Nature: Warm and dry in the second degree. *Optimum:* That which is yellow-colored and fragrant. *Usefulness:* It quenches thirst. *Dangers:* When drunk without measure. *Neutralization of the Dangers:* By eating something while drinking.
(f. 57)

57. OLD FRAGRANT WINE (VINUM VETUS ODORIFERUM)

Nature: Warm in the second degree, dry in the third. *Optimum:* The fragrant variety. *Usefulness:* Cures diseases of the eye. *Dangers:* For the senses, especially children's. *Neutralization of the Dangers:* With sour apples and the hearts of lettuce.
(f. 57v)

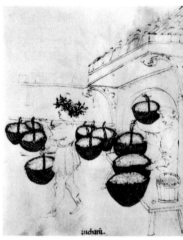

58. YELLOW COLORED WINE (VINUM CITRINUM)

Nature: Warm and dry in the second degree. *Optimum:* The clear one of the year. *Usefulness:* Removes the danger of poison. *Dangers:* Reduces the desire for coitus. *Neutralization of the Dangers:* With sour quince.
(f. 58)

59. VINEGAR (ACCETUM)

Nature: Cold in the first degree, dry in the second. *Optimum:* That which has been made from good wine. *Usefulness:* For the warmth of the gums and for the appetite. *Dangers:* For the nerves. *Neutralization of the Dangers:* With water and sugar.
(f. 58v)

60. FRESH FISH (PISCES RECENTES)

Nature: Cold and humid in the third degree. *Optimum:* Those of small size, with thin skins, and living in waters that run among stones. *Usefulness:* They fatten the body. *Dangers:* They cause thirst. *Neutralization of the Dangers:* With wine and raisins.
(f. 59)

61. SALTED FISH (PISCES SALLATI)

Nature: Warm and dry in the second degree. *Optimum:* Those not salted too long. *Dangers:* They liquefy humors and provoke collapses. *Neutralization of the Dangers:* With red wine mixed with sweet substances.
(f. 60)

62. CRAWFISH OR CRAB (GAMBARI SEU CANCRI)

Nature: Warm and dry in the secon degree. *Optimum:* Fresh ones, yellow colored. *Usefulness:* They increase co itus. *Dangers:* For sleeping. *Neutraliza tion of the Dangers:* By sprinkling the with almonds and olive oil.
(f. 61)

63. SUGAR (ZUCHARUM)

Nature: Warm in the first degree, dr in the second. *Optimum:* That which white and refined. *Usefulness:* It purifi the body and is good for the kidneys an bladder. *Dangers:* It causes thirst an moves bilious humors. *Neutralization the Dangers:* With sour pomegranates.
(f. 62)

4. HONEY (MEL)

Nature: Warm and dry in the second degree. *Optimum:* That which is still in the honeycomb. *Usefulness:* It purifies, a laxative, prevents the alteration of meats, and has humidifying properties. *Dangers:* Causes thirst and undergoes changes. *Neutralization of the Dangers:* With sour apples.
(f. 63v)

5. ROSES (ROXE)

Nature: Cold in the first degree, dry in the third. *Optimum:* The most fragrant and fresh ones. *Usefulness:* For inflamed brains. *Dangers:* They cause headaches in some people. *Neutralization of the Dangers:* With camphor.
(f. 64)

66. MUSIC PLAYING AND DANCING (SONARE ET BALARE)

Nature: To move the feet and the body in rhythm with the music. *Optimum:* When there is a strict correlation between the music and the movements of the body. *Usefulness:* By participating, looking on, or listening with joy and accord. *Dangers:* When the accord among the musical notes is lost. *Neutralization of the Dangers:* When the accord among the musical notes is restored.
(f. 64v)

67. ANGER (IRA)

Nature: Consists in the boiling of the blood in the heart. *Optimum:* The kind that engorges and restores the color that has disappeared. *Usefulness:* For paralysis and torment in the mouth. *Dangers:* For those who make illicit decisions. *Neutralization of the Dangers:* It is to be rectified by the suitableness of philosophy.
(f. 66)

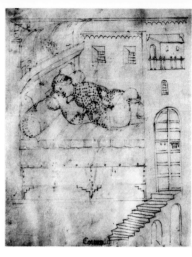

68. COITUS (COITUS)

Nature: The union of two for the purpose of emitting the sperm. *Optimum:* The kind that lasts until the sperm has been completely emitted. *Usefulness:* For the conservation of the species. *Dangers:* For those who suffer from cold and dry breathing. *Neutralization of the Dangers:* With sperm-producing foods. (f. 69v)

69. HORSEMANSHIP (EQUITATIO)

Nature: It is a kind of moderate movement. *Optimum:* When it causes perspiration. *Usefulness:* For the two things we have mentioned. *Dangers:* When it is exaggerated. *Neutralization of the Dangers:* . . . (f. 71v)

70. FENCING (LUCTATIO)

Nature: It is a moderate exercise involving two persons. *Optimum:* The kind that, once over, leaves one with a feeling of lightness. *Usefulness:* For strong bodies. *Dangers:* For the chest. *Neutralization of the Dangers:* By sleep after a bath. (f. 72)

71. TERRESTRIAL HUNTING (VENATIO TERRESTRIS)

Nature: For hunting wild game. *Optimum:* The easy kind of hunting. *Usefulness:* Thins humors. *Dangers:* Dries the body out. *Neutralization of the Dangers:* By oiling the body while bathing. (f. 72v)

72. WOOLEN CLOTHING (VESTIS DE LANA)

Nature: Warm and dry in the second degree. *Optimum:* That which is made from the very good wool from Flanders. *Usefulness:* It conducts heat. *Dangers:* It overheats. *Neutralization of the Dangers:* With linen clothing. (f. 73v)

73. SPRING WATER (AQUA FONTIUM)

Nature: Cold and humid in the fourth degree. *Optimum:* That which comes from Eastern springs. *Usefulness:* For the warm liver and for the digestion. *Dangers:* It cools and causes humid swellings. *Neutralization of the Dangers:* With baths and exercise. (f. 74)

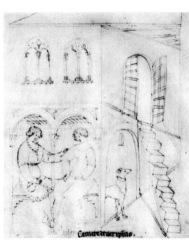

RAIN WATER (AQUA ~~L~~UUIALIS)

~~N~~ature: Cold and humid in the fourth ~~de~~gree. *Optimum:* That which has fal-~~le~~n on good land. *Usefulness:* For a ~~co~~ugh, for melancholy, for pains in the ~~ha~~nds. *Dangers:* For hoarseness, when ~~co~~ntaminated. *Neutralization of the Dan-~~ge~~rs:* . . .
~~(f. ~~74v)

SNOW AND ICE (NIS ET ~~G~~LATIES)

~~N~~ature: Cold and humid in the second ~~de~~gree. *Optimum:* That which has been ~~for~~med from sweet water. *Usefulness:* ~~Im~~proves the digestion. *Dangers:* Causes ~~cou~~ghing. *Neutralization of the Dangers:* ~~By~~ drinking it moderately.
~~(f. ~~75)

76. BATHING (BALNEUM)

Nature: Of four qualities. *Optimum:* That which is done alternately and in sweet water. *Usefulness:* For all men. *Dangers:* For acute illnesses. *Neutraliza-tion of the Dangers:* With extremely cold substances.
(f. 75v)

77. WATER OF PLEASURABLE WARMTH (AQUA DELECTABILIS CALIDITATIS)

Nature: Warm and humid in the second degree. *Optimum:* The kind that opens the pores with moderate heat or with a fever. *Usefulness:* For bodies with open pores; furthermore it lowers the tempera-ture. *Dangers:* For intestinal flow. *Neu-tralization of the Dangers:* With astrin-gent drinks.
(f. 76)

78. SALT WATER (AQUA SALSA)

Nature: Warm and dry in the second degree. *Optimum:* The nonbitter kind and nonstagnant. *Usefulness:* Frees the body. *Dangers:* Causes itching. *Neutral-ization of the Dangers:* By pouring good clay in the bath.
(f. 76v)

79. ROOMS AND THEIR AIR (CAMERE ET AER IPSIUS)

Nature: Warm, cold, humid, and dry. *Optimum:* Those with a moderate quan-tity of air and with water. *Usefulness:* For healthy persons . . . *Dangers:* For persons suffering from fainting and heart palpitations. *Neutralization of the Dan-gers:* By regulating the northerly winds.
(f. 78)

80. THE SOUTHERLY WIND (*VENTUS MERIDIONALIS*)

Nature: Warm in the second degree and dry in the third. *Optimum:* The one that sweeps across lands with good air. *Usefulness:* For the chest. *Dangers:* Dulls the senses. *Neutralization of the Dangers:* With baths.
(f. 78v)

81. THE NORTHERLY WIND (*VENTUS SEPTENTRIONALIS*)

Nature: Cold in the third degree, dry in the second. *Optimum:* The one that sweeps across sweet waters. *Usefulness:* It sharpens the senses. *Dangers:* For the chest and cough. *Neutralization of the Dangers:* With baths and heavy clothing.
(f. 79)

82. THE WESTERLY WIND (*VENTUS OCCIDENTALIS*)

Nature: Warm and dry in the second degree. *Optimum:* That coming from the North. *Usefulness:* Aids digestion. *Dangers:* Causes shivering and colds. *Neutralization of the Dangers:* With heating.
(f. 79v)

83. THE EASTERLY WIND (*VENTUS ORIENTALIS*)

Nature: Warm. *Optimum:* The one that sweeps over waters and brings rain. *Usefulness:* Enhances the spirit. *Dangers:* For diseases of the eyes and the heart. *Neutralization of the Dangers:* With river water.
(f. 80)

84. SPRING (*VER*)

Nature: Of moderate humidity in second degree. *Optimum:* Its mid period. *Usefulness:* To all animals a blossoming plants. *Dangers:* For fil bodies. *Neutralization of the Dange By cleansing the body.
(f. 80v)

85. SUMMER (*ESTAS*)

Nature: Of moderate warmth in third degree. *Optimum:* Its initial pe od. *Usefulness:* Dissolves superfluiti *Dangers:* Prevents digestion and cau bilious humors. *Neutralization of Dangers:* With cooling and moist su stances.
(f. 81)

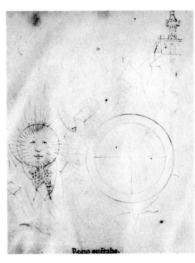

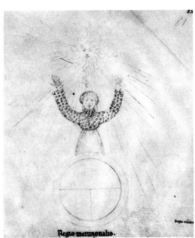

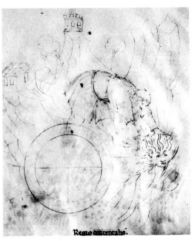

6. AUTUMN (AUTUNPNUS)

Nature: Of moderate warmth. *Optimum:* Its middle period. *Usefulness:* When one proceeds gradually toward the opposites. *Dangers:* For moderate temperaments. *Neutralization of the Dangers:* With moistening substances poured in the bath.
(f. 81v)

7. WINTER (HIEMPS)

Nature: Cold and humid. *Optimum:* The period closest to Spring. *Usefulness:* Betters digestion. *Dangers:* Generates phlegm. *Neutralization of the Dangers:* By heating foods and water, with heavy clothing or baths.
(f. 82)

88. NORTHERLY REGION (REGIO SEPTENTRIONALIS)

Nature: Cold and dry. *Optimum:* That which possesses good water and fertile topsoil. *Usefulness:* Inspires strength and prudence. *Dangers:* For chests of small dimensions. *Neutralization of the Dangers:* By regulating one's sojourns with great care.
(f. 82v)

89. SOUTHERLY REGION (REGIO MERIDIONALIS)

Nature: Warm and humid. *Optimum:* That which is far from the sea and near the North. *Usefulness:* Produces a feeling of greater spaciousness. *Dangers:* For those sick with smallpox and measles. *Neutralization of the Dangers:* By comforting the head and the stomach.
(f. 83)

90. EASTERLY REGION (REGIO ORIENTALIS)

Nature: Temperate. *Optimum:* The Northerly and Southerly zones adjacent to one another. *Usefulness:* For almost all temperaments. *Dangers:* Being too luminous. *Neutralization of the Dangers:* With heavy foods.
(f. 83v)

91. WESTERLY REGION (REGIO OCCIDENTALIS)

Nature: Of variable temperature. *Optimum:* . . . *Usefulness:* . . . manifestations . . . *Dangers:* Causes deviations in temperaments. *Neutralization of the Dangers:* With substances that rectify that process.
(f. 84)

B. THE TACUINA OF PARIS, VIENNA, ROUEN, AND THE THEATRUM IN ROME

92. ALBULKASEM DE BALDAC, SON OF THE PHYSICIAN HABADUM, COMPOSED THIS BOOK.

We are listing here all the names of those men of wisdom mentioned in this book and are designating each by the first letter of his name.

Hippocrates with a Greek Y, Galen by G, Rufus by R, Dioscorides by D, Paulus by P. Orebasius by O, Theodorus by T. Johannes by Jo, Maserice by Ma, Jesus by Je, Scirvindi by Schi, Rasis by Ra, Muscia by Mn, Johannicus by a Latin J, Ysach by Ys, Albuscasem by Al.

Keep in mind that medicine speaks of four degrees, that is, 1st, 2nd, 3rd, 4th, and no more.

(*Paris,* f. 1)

93. *ELLBOCHASIM DE BALDACH*

Tacuinum Sanitatis in medicina explains the six things necessary to clarify the benefits of foods, of drinks, and of clothing, their dangers and the neutralization of those dangers, according to the advice of the wisest men among the ancients.

Tacuinum Sanitatis is about the six things that are needed by every man for the daily preservation of his health, about their exact use and their effects. The first is the treatment of the air, which concerns the heart. The second is the right use of foods and drinks. The third is the correct application of movement and rest. The fourth is the problem of prohibition of the body from sleep or excessive wakefulness. The fifth is the correct use of elimination and retention of humors. The sixth is the regulating of the person by moderating joy, anger, fear, and distress. The secret of the preservation of health, in fact, will be the proper balance of all these elements. Disturbing the balance of these six elements causes the diseases which the glorious and most exalted God permits. Included in these six classifications are many varieties which are very useful and whose nature, God willing, we shall explain. Furthermore, we shall speak of the choices which are suitable to each person on the basis of his constitution and age, and shall insert all these elements into simple tables because the discussions of the sages and the discordances in many different books may bore the reader. In fact, men desire from science nothing but the benefits, not the arguments but the definitions. Accordingly, our intention in this book is to shorten long-winded discourses and synthesize the various ideas. However, it is also our intention not to neglect the advice of the ancients. In this book, therefore, we shall include only orderly catalogues, the abbreviations of the interlocutors, and deductions from the proofs which sustain the validity of words. We do not intend to follow men's ideas according to the divergences of their opinions. We invoke God's assistance so that He may guide our minds justly, since human nature is hardly immune from error, and our entire work corresponds to our modest intention in the pursuit of which may God assist and guide us according to his will.

(*Vienna,* f. 4)

94. BOOK OF MASTER UBUBCHASYM DE BALDACH

Theatrum Sanitatis is about the six things that are necessary for every man in the daily preservation of his
health, about their exact use and their effects. The first
is the treatment of air, which every day concerns the
heart. The second is the just use of foods and drinks.
The third is the correct use of movement and rest. The
fourth is the problem of prohibition of the body from
sleep or excessive wakefulness. The fifth is the correct
use of the elimination and retention of humors. The
sixth is the regulation of the person by moderating joy,
anger, fear, and distress. The secret of the preservation
of health, in fact, will be in the proper balance of all
these elements, since disturbing this balance causes the
illnesses which are permitted by the glorious and most
exalted God. Included under these six classifications
are many very useful varieties whose nature, God willing, we shall explain. We shall also speak of the choices
suitable to each person as dictated by his constitution
and age, and will include all these elements in simple
tables because the discussions of the ancients and the
discordances among so many diverse books may be bore
the reader. From science, in fact, men desire only the
benefits, not the arguments but the definitions. Accordingly, our intention in this book is to shorten long-
winded discourses and synthesize the various ideas.
Our intention, however, is also that of not neglecting
the advice of the ancients.
(*Casanatense*, f. I)

95. THE PHYSICIAN SPEAKS

The *Tacuinum Sanitatis* is about the six things that are necessary for every man in the daily preservation of his health, about their correct uses and their effects. The first is the treatment of air, which concerns the heart. The second is the right use of foods and drinks. The third is the correct use of movement and rest. The fourth is the problem of prohibition of the body from sleep or excessive wakefulness. The fifth is the correct use of elimination and retention of humors. The sixth is the regulating of the person by moderating joy, anger, fear, and distress. The secret of the preservation of health, in fact, will be in the proper balance of all these elements, since it is the disturbance of this balance that causes the illnesses which the glorious and most exalted God permits. Listed under these six classifications are many very useful varieties whose nature, God willing, we shall explain. We shall speak, furthermore, about the choices suitable to each person owing to his constitution and age, and shall include all these elements in the form of simple tables because the discussions of the sages and the discordances in many different books may bore the reader. Men, in fact, desire from science nothing else but the benefits, not the arguments but the definitions. Accordingly, our intention in this book is to shorten long-winded discourses and synthesize the various ideas. Our intention also, however, is not to neglect the advice of the ancients.

(*Rouen*, f. 1)

6. GARLIC (*ALEA*)

Nature: Warm in the second degree, dry [in] the third. *Optimum:* The kind that [d]oes not have too pungent a smell. *Use[f]ulness:* Against poisons. *Dangers:* For [th]e faculty of expulsion, and the brain. *[N]eutralization of the Dangers:* With vin[e]gar and oil.
[C]asanatense, f. XLV)

7. GARLIC (*ALEA*)

[N]ature: Warm in the fourth degree, dry [in] the third. *Optimum:* The kind that [d]oes not have too pungent a smell. *Use[f]ulness:* Against poisons. *Dangers:* For [th]e faculty of expulsion, and the brain. *[N]eutralization of the Dangers:* With vin[e]gar and oil.
[R]ouen, f. 23)

98. SWEET ALMONDS (*AMIGDALE DULCES*)

Nature: Warm and dry in the second degree. *Optimum:* The large and sweet ones. *Usefulness:* Consumed before drinking, they prevent drunkenness and anxiety; furthermore, they remove freckles. *Dangers:* They are harmful for the intestines. *Neutralization of the Dangers:* With sugar and poppies. *Effects:* They produce humors that facilitate digestion. They are particularly good for cold temperaments, for old people, in Winter, and in the Northerly regions.
(*Vienna,* f. 18v)

99. DUCKS AND GEESE (*ANATES ET ANSERES*)

Nature: (According to Hippocrates), warm and dry in the second degree. *Optimum:* Those which stayed quietly in their nests after hatching. *Usefulness:* They fatten lean people. *Dangers:* They fill the body with superfluities. *Neutralization of the Dangers:* Rubbing them with oil and filling them with many spices.
(*Paris,* f. 71v)

100. DUCKS AND GEESE (*ANATES ET ANSERES*)

Nature: Warm and dry in the second degree. *Optimum:* Those which stayed quietly in their nests after hatching. *Usefulness:* They fatten melancholy people. *Dangers:* They fill the body with superfluities. *Neutralization of the Dangers:* By blowing borax down their throats before killing them.
(*Casanatense,* f. CXXXII)

101. DILL (*ANETUM*)

Nature: Warm and dry in the third degree. *Optimum:* That which is green and fresh. *Usefulness:* Its juice helps the stomach. *Dangers:* For the kidneys; besides, it causes nausea in the stomach with its substance. *Neutralization of the Dangers:* With *limocellis* (juice of small lemons?).
(*Paris,* f. 40v)

102. DILL *(ANETI)*

Nature: Warm and dry in the third degree. *Optimum:* That which is green and fresh. *Usefulness:* It is good for the stomach that is rich in humors. *Dangers:* For the kidneys, and it nauseates the stomach with its substance. *Neutralization of the Dangers:* With *lemoncelis* (juice of small lemons?).
(Casanatense, f. LVII)

103. CELERY *(APIUM)*

Nature: (According to Albulcasem), warm and cold in the first degree. *Optimum:* The garden variety. *Usefulness:* Removes obstructions. *Dangers:* Causes headaches. *Neutralization of the Dangers:* With lettuce.
(Paris, f. 28v)

104. CELERY *(APIUM)*

Nature: Warm and dry in the first degree. *Optimum:* The garden variety. *Usefulness:* Removes obstructions. *Dangers:* Causes headaches. *Neutralization of the Dangers:* With lettuce. *Effects:* It is moderately nourishing and is good for cold temperaments, for old people, in Winter, and in cold regions.
(Vienna, f. 30)

105. BARLEY WATER *(AQUA ORDEI)*

Nature: (According to Hippocrates), co and dry in the second degree. *Optimun* That which has been thoroughly boile *Usefulness:* For an inflamed liver. *Da gers:* For cold intestines. *Neutralizatio of the Dangers:* With rose-colored suga
(Paris, f. 52)

106. BARLEY WATER *(AQUA ORDEY)*

Nature: Cold and dry in the second d gree. *Optimum:* That which has be thoroughly boiled and is mild. *Usef ness:* For the inflamed stomach. *Dange* It is harmful for cold intestines. *Neutra zation of the Dangers:* With sugar. *E fects:* Temperate blood. It is suitable f warm temperaments, for young peop in Summer, and in Southerly regions.
(Vienna, f. 45)

7. SALT WATER (AQUA SALSA)

Nature: Warm and dry in the second degree. *Optimum:* The flowing, nonbitter and. *Usefulness:* It frees the belly and en dries. *Dangers:* Causes itching and harmful for the eyes. *Neutralization of e Dangers:* By mixing it with good clay d taking a bath after drinking it. *Efcts:* Thirst and occlusions. It is more itable for cold and humid temperaents, for very old people, in Winter, d in cold regions.
Vienna, f. 88)

08. APRICOTS (ARMONACA)

ature: . . . *Optimum:* Those from Arenia, that is, well ripened. *Usefulness:* hey cause vomiting. *Dangers:* They ool the stomach noticeably. *Neutralizaon of the Dangers:* By vomiting.
Paris, f. 7v)

09. APRICOTS (ARMONIACHA)

ature: Cold and humid in the second egree. *Optimum:* Those from Armenia nu barni.(?) *Usefulness:* They cause voming. *Dangers:* They cool the stomach nd spoil very easily. *Neutralization of he Dangers:* By vomiting. *Effects:* Phlegiatic blood. They are suitable for temeraments of medium warmth, for young eople, at the beginning of Summer, and the Eastern regions.
Vienna, f. 9v)

110. AUTUMN (AUPTUMNUS)

Nature: Somewhat temperate. *Optimum:* Its middle period. *Usefulness:* When one proceeds gradually toward opposites. *Dangers:* Moderates the . . . *Neutralization of the Dangers:* With moistening substances poured into the bath.
(*Paris,* f. 103v)

111. AUTUMN (AUTUMPNUS)

Nature: Somewhat temperate. *Optimum:* Its middle period. *Usefulness:* By proceeding gradually toward opposites. *Dangers:* For temperate constitutions. *Neutralization of the Dangers:* With moistening substances poured into the bath.
(*Casanatense,* f. CII)

Nature: They must be of modera warmth. *Optimum:* Those with a ten perature similar to that at the end Spring. *Usefulness:* They reawaken t faculties made drowsy by the cold a *Dangers:* They cause thirst and allo food not properly digested to pa through. *Neutralization of the Danger* By placing them toward the Northerl side. They are suitable above all to co temperaments, to very old people, extremely frigid temperatures, and mountainous regions.
(*Vienna,* f. 97v)

112. CHICK PEA SOUP
(*BRODIUM CICERUM*)

Nature: (According to Albulcasem), warm and humid in the second degree. *Optimum:* That prepared with chick peas, broad beans, and sweet milk. *Usefulness:* For paralysis. *Dangers:* For those suffering from bile. *Neutralization of the Dangers:* . . .
(*Paris,* f. 46)

113. SUMMER ROOMS (*CAMERE ESTUALES*)

Nature: . . . *Optimum:* Those with a Spring temperature. *Usefulness:* They bring the constitutional elements and the digestion to the same temperature. *Dangers:* . . . *Neutralization of the Dangers:* With baths.
(*Paris,* f. 99)

114. SUMMER ROOMS (*CAMERAE ESTIUALES*)

Nature: Moderately cold and humid. *Optimum:* Those with a Spring temperature. *Usefulness:* They bring the constitutional elements and the digestion to the same temperature. *Dangers:* Prevents the dissolution of Summer. *Neutralization of the Dangers:* With baths.
(*Casanatense,* f. CLXXXVII)

115. WINTER ROOMS (*CAMERE HYMALES*)

Nature: Moderately warm. *Optimum:* Those with a temperature similar to that at the end of Spring. *Usefulness:* They reawaken the faculties rendered drowsy by cold air. *Dangers:* They cause thirst and let food pass through although not thoroughly digested. *Neutralization of the Dangers:* By placing them toward the Northerly side.
(*Paris,* f. 98v)

117. CAPERS (*CAPARI*)

Nature: Warm in the third degree, dry in the second. *Optimum:* Those which are fresh and tender. *Usefulness:* They reduce the quantity of the urine. *Dangers:* They reduce blood and sperm. . . . *Neutralization of the Dangers:* With Vinegar.
(*Paris*, f. 39)

118. CAPERS (*CAPARI*)

Nature: Warm in the second degree. *Optimum:* The full ones, not yet open, from Alexandria. *Usefulness:* They help the stomach and the appetite, remove occlusions of the liver and of the spleen, and kill worms. *Dangers:* They are difficult to digest. *Neutralization of the Dangers:* By cooking them with oil, vinegar, and aromatic spices. *Effects:* They heat the blood and are more suitable to cold temperaments, old people, children, in Winter, and in cold regions. But, if prepared as described above, they are good for all temperaments and ages and in every region.
(*Vienna*, f. 24v)

119. CAPERS (*CAPARI*)

Nature: Warm in the third degree, dry in the second. *Optimum:* Those which are tender and fresh. *Usefulness:* They reduce the quantity of the urine. *Dangers:* They reduce the blood and the sperm. *Neutralization of the Dangers:* With vinegar.
(*Casanatense*, f. XLII)

120. RAM MEAT (*CARNES ARIETUM*)

Nature: Warm and humid in the first degree. *Optimum:* Those fattened during the year. *Usefulness:* For a temperate stomach. *Dangers:* For those suffering habitually from nausea. *Neutralization of the Dangers:* With astringent broths.
(*Paris*, f. 61v)

121. RAM MEAT (*CARNES ARIETUM*)

Nature: Warm and humid in the first degree. *Optimum:* Those fattened during the year. *Usefulness:* For a temperate stomach. *Dangers:* For those suffering habitually from nausea. *Neutralization of the Dangers:* With astringent broths.
(*Casanatense*, f. CXXXVIII)

122. GOAT MEAT AND LAMB (*CARNES CAPRORUM ET PULPE EDORUM*)

Nature: (According to Johannes), of moderate warmth in the second degree. *Optimum:* The red meat of lamb, tending toward the brown. *Usefulness:* Quickly digestible. *Dangers:* For colic, when roasted. *Neutralization of the Dangers:* With foods mixed with honey.
(*Paris*, f. 62.)

123. ROASTED MEAT (*CARNES SUFRYXE*)

Nature: Warm and dry. *Optimum:* Well roasted. *Usefulness:* For bodies and stomachs of a humid nature. *Dangers:* Causes thirst. *Neutralization of the Dangers:* With acidulous wine. *Effects:* It sharpens the blood and is more suitable to cold and humid temperaments, to old people, in Winter, and in Northerly regions.
(*Vienna*, f. 75v)

124. ROASTED MEAT (*CARNES SUFRITE*)

Nature: Warm and dry. *Optimum:* that which is well roasted and moist. *Usefulness:* Makes one phlegmatic. *Dangers:* Causes thirst. *Neutralization of the Dangers:* With good wine of recent vintage.
(*Casanatense*, f. CXLIV)

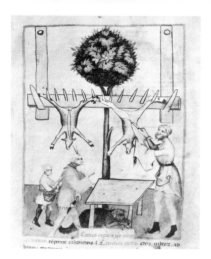

125. COW MEAT AND CAMEL MEAT (*CARNES VACINAE ET CAMELORUM*)

Nature: Warm and dry in the second degree. *Optimum:* That which comes from young and free animals. *Usefulness:* For those performing heavy work and those suffering from bile disfunctions.
Dangers: For people sick from melancholia. *Neutralization of the Dangers:* With ginger and pepper.
(*Casanatense*, f. CXLII)

126. VEAL (*CARNES UITULORUM*)

Nature: Of moderate warmth in the second degree. *Optimum:* That which comes from animals newly born. *Usefulness:* For those engaged in heavy work. *Dangers:* For people suffering from bile disfunctions. *Neutralization of the Dangers:* With exercise and baths.
(*Paris*, f. 62v)

127. VEAL (CARNES UITULORUM)

Nature: Warm and moist in the first degree. *Optimum:* That which comes from animals newly born. *Usefulness:* For those performing heavy work. *Dangers:* For people suffering from disfunctions of the spleen. *Neutralization of the Dangers:* With exercise and baths. *Effects:* Very nourishing. It is more suitable to warm temperaments, to young people, in Spring, and in Southerly regions. According to Galen, veal is better than ram. (*Vienna,* f. 73v)

128. FRESH CHEESE (CASEUS RECENS)

Nature: (According to Albulcasem), cold and humid. *Optimum:* That which is of moderate warmth and is made from the milk of a healthy animal. *Usefulness:* Softens the body and fattens it. *Dangers:* Causes occlusions. *Neutralization of the Dangers:* With walnuts, almonds, and honey.
(*Paris,* f. 58v)

129. OLD CHEESE (CASEUM VETUS)

Nature: Warm and cold. *Optimum:* The fatty, tasty kind. *Usefulness:* It soothes the flux when roasted. *Dangers:* For gallstones and kidney stones. *Neutralization of the Dangers:* By eating it between courses. (*Paris,* f. 59v)

130. CHESTNUTS (CASTANEE)

Nature: (According to Albulcasem), warm and dry in the second degree. *Optimum:* . . . *Usefulness:* They are very nourishing when cooked; raw . . . *Dangers:* They are difficult to digest. *Neutralization of the ·Dangers:* Cooked in water and served with good wine.
(*Paris,* f. 11)

131. CHESTNUTS (CASTANEE)

Nature: Warm in the first degree, dry in the second. *Optimum:* The marrons of Brianza, well ripened. *Usefulness:* They are favorable to coitus and are very nourishing. *Dangers:* They inflate and cause headaches. *Neutralization of the Dangers:* By cooking them in water.
(*Casanatense,* f. XXIV)

132. DATES (*CEPHALONES IDEST DACTILI*)

Nature: (According to Johannes), cold in the first degree, dry in the second. *Optimum:* The sweet and fresh ones. *Usefulness:* They help the intestines. *Dangers:* For the chest and the throat. *Neutralization of the Dangers:* With dates and a honeycomb. (*Paris*, f. 16)

133. DATES (*CEFALONES IDEST DATILI*)

Nature: Cold in the first degree, dry in the second. *Optimum:* The sweet and fresh ones. *Usefulness:* They help the intestines. *Dangers:* For the chest and the throat. *Neutralization of the Dangers:* With dates and a honeycomb. (*Casanatense*, f. XXXI)

134. ONIONS (*CEPE*)

Nature: (According to Rasis), warm in the fourth degree, moist in the third. *Optimum:* The white ones which are watery and juicy. *Usefulness:* They are diuretic and facilitate coitus. *Dangers:* They cause headaches. *Neutralization of the Dangers:* With vinegar and milk. (*Paris*, f. 24v)

135. ONIONS (*CEPE*)

Nature: Warm in the fourth degree, moist in the third degree, dry at other times. *Optimum:* The white ones that are watery and juicy. *Usefulness:* They soften the nature, provoke urine, increase coitus, and sharpen the eyesight. *Dangers:* They cause headaches. *Neutralization of the Dangers:* With vinegar and milk. *Effects:* They generate milk and sperm and are good for cold temperaments, for very old people, in Winter, and in Northerly regions. (*Vienna*, f. 25v)

136. SOUR CHERRIES (*CEREXA ACCETOSA*)

Nature: . . . *Optimum:* The sweet on with thin skins. *Usefulness:* for a phl matic stomach burdened with superf ities. *Dangers:* They are digested slow *Neutralization of the Dangers:* By eati them on an empty stomach. (*Paris*, f. 9v)

137. SOUR CHERRIES (*CEROSA ACETOSA*)

Nature: Cold in the third degree, in the second. *Optimum:* Those wh are thoroughly sour. *Usefulness:* Agai acute crises of the bile; they also dry the superfluities in the stomach and s tain it. *Dangers:* For the teeth and nerves. *Neutralization of the Dange* With sweet almonds and raisins. *Effe* They generate good chyme and are b ter for warm temperaments, for you people and children, in Summer, and Southerly regions. (*Vienna*, f. 12)

138. SWEET CHERRIES (CEREXA DULCIA)

Nature: Cold and humid in the first degree. *Optimum:* Ripe ones. *Usefulness:* They moisten the stomach and soften the abdomen. *Dangers:* For the stomach, if abused. *Neutralization of the Dangers:* With sweet wine.
Paris, f. 9)

139. QUINCE (CITONIA)

Nature: Cold and dry in the second degree. *Optimum:* Those which are large and full. *Usefulness:* They cheer people up and cause excitement. *Dangers:* For colic. *Neutralization of the Dangers:* With dates mixed with honey.
Casanatense, f. IX)

140. CHATTING (CONFABULATOR)

Nature: It induces sleep. *Optimum:* That which is suitable to the nature of the person who wishes to sleep. *Usefulness:* For those who delight in such an endeavor. *Dangers:* It causes boredom. *Neutralization of the Dangers:* By sleeping.
(*Paris,* f. 90)

141. WATERMELONS AND CUCUMBERS (COCUMERES ET CITRULI)

Nature: Cold and humid in the second degree. *Optimum:* Full ones which have not yet turned yellow. *Usefulness:* For burning fevers and to provoke urination. *Dangers:* They cause stomach aches and pains in the side. *Neutralization of the Dangers:* With honey and oil. *Effects:* They generate watery blood, which is not praiseworthy, and are more suitable for warm temperaments, for young people, in Summer, and in warm regions.
(*Vienna,* f. 23v)

142. WATERMELONS AND CUCUMBERS (CUCUMERES ET CITRULI)

Nature: Cold and humid in the third degree. *Optimum:* . . . full. *Usefulness:* Against burning fevers and to provoke urination. *Dangers:* They cause pains in the sides and in the stomach. *Neutralization of the Dangers:* With honey and oil.
(*Casanatense,* f. XL)

143. SQUASH (CUCURBITE)

Nature: (According to Galen), cold and humid in the second degree. *Optimum:* Those which are fresh and green. *Usefulness:* They quench thirst. *Dangers:* They are altered and assimilated too quickly. *Neutralization of the Dangers:* With salted water and mustard.
(*Paris,* f. 36v)

144. SQUASH (*CUCURBITE*)

Nature: Cold and humid in the second degree. *Optimum:* The fresh and green ones. *Usefulness:* For quenching thirst. *Dangers:* They are altered and descend quickly. *Neutralization of the Dangers:* With salted water and mustard. (*Casanatense,* f. XXXVIII)

145. ELECAMPANE (*ENULA*)

Nature: Warm and dry in the second degree. *Optimum:* Its root. *Usefulness:* It relieves the opening to the stomach and purifies the chest. *Dangers:* Causes headaches. *Neutralization of the Dangers:* By preparing meals containing coriander seeds. (*Paris,* f. 35)

146. ELECAMPANE (*ENULA*)

Nature: Warm and dry in the second degree. *Optimum:* The root of the field elecampane. *Usefulness:* Fortifies the opening to the stomach and purifies the chest. *Dangers:* Causes headaches. *Neutralization of the Dangers:* By preparing meals containing coriander seeds. (*Casanatense,* f. LXIV)

147. LIVER (*EPATA ANIMALIUM*)

Nature: (According to Albulcasen warm and humid in the second degr *Optimum:* That which comes from geese. *Usefulness:* For those who suf from night blindness (goat liver is p ticularly useful). *Dangers:* For ti stomachs. *Neutralization of the Dange* With oil and salt. (*Paris,* f. 73v)

148. LIVER (*EPATA ANIMALIUM*)

Nature: Warm and humid in the seco degree. *Optimum:* That which com from geese fattened on milk and pas then that of chicken, then that of pi fattened on figs. *Usefulness:* For th who suffer from night blindness (g liver is particularly indicated). *Dange* It tires the stomach since it is difficult digest. *Neutralization of the Dange* With oil and salt. *Effects:* It purifies t blood and is more suitable for cold te peraments, for young people, in Wint and in Northerly regions. (*Vienna,* f. 80)

149. HORSEBACK RIDING (EQUITATORES)

Nature: It represents a variety of moderate movement. *Optimum:* That which causes perspiration. *Usefulness:* . . . *Dangers:* . . . *Neutralization of the Dangers:* With moist substances.
(*Paris,* f. 93)

150. WATERCRESS (RUCULA)

Nature: (According to Johannes), warm and humid in the first degree. *Optimum:* That whose flavor is not too strong. *Usefulness:* Augments the sperm and coitus. *Dangers:* Causes migraines. *Neutralization of the Dangers:* With a salad of escarole and vinegar.
(*Paris,* f. 21v)

151. GARDEN NASTURTIUMS (ERUCA ET NASTURTIUM)

Nature: Warm and humid in the first degree. *Optimum:* Those which have the best flavor. *Usefulness:* Augment the sperm and coitus. *Dangers:* Cause migraines. *Neutralization of the Dangers:* With a salad of escarole and vinegar. *Effects:* They generate sharp blood and are more suitable for cold temperaments, for old people, in Winter, and in the Northerly regions.
(*Vienna,* f. 30v)

152. GARDEN NASTURTIUMS (ERUCA ET NASTURCIUM)

Nature: Warm and humid in the first degree. *Optimum:* Those which have a stronger flavor. *Usefulness:* Augment the sperm and coitus. *Dangers:* Cause migraines. *Neutralization of the Dangers:* With a salad of escarole and vinegar.
(*Casanatense,* f. LIV)

153. SUMMER (ESTAS)

Nature: Of moderate warmth in the second degree. *Optimum:* Its initial period. *Usefulness:* Dissolves superfluities. *Dangers:* Hinders the digestion because of the bile. *Neutralization of the Dangers:* With humid and cooling substances.
(*Casanatense.* f. XLV)

154. PHEASANTS (FASIANI)

Nature: Of moderate warmth and dry.
Optimum: Those fattened on oats and
which are beginning to sing. *Usefulness:*
For moderately warm natures. *Dangers:*
They prolong quartan fever. *Neutraliza-
tion of the Dangers:* With oily sub-
stances.
(*Paris,* f. 67)

155. PHEASANTS (FAXIANI)

Nature: Warm and dry. *Optimum:* Those
fattened on oats and which are beginning to sing. *Usefulness:* For moderately
warm natures. *Dangers:* They prolong
quartan fever. *Neutralization of the Dangers:* With oily substances.
(*Casanatense,* f. CXXX)

156. FENNEL (FENICULUM)

Nature: Warm and dry in the first ⌐
gree. *Optimum:* The domestic varie
Usefulness: For the eyesight and ⌐
fevers. *Dangers:* For the menstrual flo
Neutralization of the Dangers: With .
and carobs.
(*Paris,* f. 41)

157. FENNEL (FENICULUS)

Nature: Warm in the third degree, ⌐
in the second. At other times, warm a
dry in the second degree. *Optimu*
The domestic variety, fresh, with ⌐
strong taste. *Usefulness:* For the e⌐
purifies the eyesight, stimulates milk a
urine flow, diminishes flatulence. *D*
gers: It is digested slowly. *Neutralizat*
of the Dangers: By chewing it well. ⌐
fects: Generates bilious humors. It ⌐
suitable for cold temperaments, for ⌐
people, in Winter when it is possible
find it, in cold regions and in all oth⌐
in which it grows.
(*Vienna,* f. 41v)

158. FIGS *(FICHUS)*

Nature: Warm and humid in the second degree. *Optimum:* The white, peeled kind. *Usefulness:* Cleans the kidneys and reduces sediments. *Dangers:* Inflates and fattens. *Neutralization of the Dangers:* With sour syrup or salted water. *(Casanatense,* f. II)

159. WHEAT *(FURMENTUM)*

Nature: (According to Albulcasem), warm and humid in the second degree. *Optimum:* The large and heavy grains. *Usefulness:* Opens ulcerations. *Dangers:* Causes occlusions. *Neutralization of the Dangers:* By cooking it well. *(Paris,* f. 46v)

160. ROOSTERS *(GALLI)*

Nature: Warm and dry in the second degree. *Optimum:* Those of moderate voice. *Usefulness:* For sufferers from colic. *Dangers:* For the stomach. *Neutralization of the Dangers:* By tiring the animal before slaughtering it. *(Paris,* f. 68v)

161. ROOSTERS *(GALLI)*

Nature: Warm and dry in the second degree. *Optimum:* Those of moderate voice. *Usefulness:* For sufferers from colic. *Dangers:* For the stomach. *Neutralization of the Dangers:* By tiring the animal before slaughtering it. *(Casanatense,* f. CXXIII)

162. CRAYFISH *(CAMBARI)*

Nature: Warm and dry in the second degree. *Optimum:* The fresh, lemon-colored ones. *Usefulness:* They augment coitus. *Dangers:* For sleep. *Neutralization of the Dangers:* By pouring almonds and olive oil over them. *(Paris,* f. 80)

163. CRAYFISH *(GAMBARI)*

Nature: Warm and dry in the second degree. *Optimum:* The fresh, lemon-colored ones. *Usefulness:* They augment coitus. *Dangers:* For sleep. *Neutralization of the Dangers:* By pouring almond oil over them. *(Casanatense,* f. CLX)

164. ACORNS (GLANDES)

Nature: Cold in the second degree, dry in the third. *Optimum:* Those that are fresh, large, and full. *Usefulness:* They help the retentive faculties. *Dangers:* They interrupt menstruation. *Neutralization of the Dangers:* By eating them roasted and with sugar.
(*Casanatense*, f. XX)

165. SOUR POMEGRANATES (*GRANATA ACETOSA*)

Nature: . . . humid in the first degree. *Optimum:* Those that are very juicy. *Usefulness:* For an inflamed liver. *Dangers:* For the chest and the voice. *Neutralization of the Dangers:* With foods mixed with honey.
(*Paris*, f. 5v)

166. SOUR POMEGRANATES (*GRANATA ACETOSA*)

Nature: Cold. *Optimum:* Those that are very watery. *Usefulness:* For an inflamed liver. *Dangers:* For the chest. *Neutralization of the Dangers:* With foods mixed with honey. *Effects:* They generate a moderate chyme and are suitable for warm temperaments, for young people, in Summer, and in warm regions.
(*Vienna*, f. 7v)

167. SWEET POMEGRANATES (*GRANATA DULCIA*)

Nature: (According to Maserice), warm in the first degree and humid in the second. *Optimum:* . . . *Usefulness:* For coughing and coitus. *Dangers:* They produce swellings. *Neutralization of the Dangers:* With sour pomegranates.
(*Paris*, f. 5)

168. SWEET POMEGRANATES (*GRANATA DULCIA*)

Nature: Warm in the first degree, humid in the second. *Optimum:* The sweet large ones. *Usefulness:* For coughing and coitus. *Dangers:* They cause swelling. *Neutralization of the Dangers:* With sour pomegranates.
(*Casanatense*, f. VII)

169. CRANES (*GRUES*)

Nature: (According to Theodorus) warm and dry in the second degree. *Optimum:* Those captured with a hunting falcon. *Usefulness:* For those who engage in heavy work. *Dangers:* They are digested badly. *Neutralization of the Dangers:* By cooking them with warm spices.
(*Paris*, f. 70v)

170. CRANES (GRUES)

Nature: Warm and dry in the second degree. *Optimum:* Those captured with a hunting falcon. *Usefulness:* For those who engage in heavy work. *Dangers:* They are digested badly. *Neutralization of the Dangers:* By cooking them with warm spices.
(*Casanatense*, f. CXXXIII)

171. WINTER (HYEMPS)

Nature: Cold and humid. *Optimum:* When it is closer to Spring. *Usefulness:* Improves digestion. *Dangers:* Generates phlegm. *Neutralization of the Dangers:* With heating, fire, heavy clothing, and baths.
(*Casanatense*, f. CIII)

172. ORGAN MEATS OR TRIPE (VISCERA SIVE BUSECHA)

Nature: (According to Albulcasem), cold and dry in the second degree. *Optimum:* Those of the ram. *Usefulness:* For people whose food ferments in their stomachs. *Dangers:* For varicosities. *Neutralization of the Dangers:* By seasoning prepared with ginger and pepper.
(*Paris*, f. 74v)

173. ENTRAILS OR TRIPE (INTESTINA IDEST BUSECHA)

Nature: Cold and dry in the second degree. *Optimum:* Those of the ram. *Usefulness:* For people whose food ferments in their stomachs. *Dangers:* For varicosities. *Neutralization of the Dangers:* By seasoning prepared with ginger and pepper.
(*Casanatense*, f. CLVI)

174. ANGER (IRA)

Nature: The boiling of the blood in the heart. *Optimum:* The kind that enlarges and restores the evanescent color. *Usefulness:* For paralysis and the torment of the mouth. *Dangers:* For those who give in to illicit decisions. *Neutralization of the Dangers:* With the convenience of philosophy.
(*Paris*, f. 88)

175. ANGER (IRA)

Nature: It is the boiling of the blood near the heart due to a desire for vengeance. *Optimum:* The kind that pushes the blood outward, fills the veins, enlarges and restores the color to the complexion. *Usefulness:* For sufferers from paralysis. *Dangers:* For those who consent to illicit decisions; by its multiplication it causes, in fact, yellow coloring, trembling, fever, and anxiety. *Neutralization of the Dangers:* With the convenience of philosophy and customs. It is more suitable to cold temperaments, to very old people, in Winter, and in cold regions.
(*Vienna,* f. 98v)

176. ANGER (IRA)

Nature: The boiling of the blood in the heart. *Optimum:* The kind that enlarges and restores the evanescent color. *Usefulness:* For paralysis and pains in the mouth. *Dangers:* For those who give in to illicit decisions. *Neutralization of the Dangers:* With the convenience of philosophy.
(*Casanatense,* f. CXC)

177. COAGULATED MILK (LAC COAGULATUM)

Nature: Cold and humid. *Optimum:* That which comes from young animals. *Usefulness:* Against swellings of the stomach. *Dangers:* Weighs the stomach down. *Neutralization of the Dangers:* With castor sugar and salt. *Effects:* It generates phlegmatic blood. It is suitable for warm temperaments, for young people, in Summer, and in Southerly regions.
(*Vienna,* f. 61v)

178. SWEET MILK (LAC DULCE)

Nature: (According to Albulcasem), o moderate warmth. *Optimum:* That which comes from young sheep. *Usefulness* For the chest and lungs. *Dangers:* Fo fevers. *Neutralization of the Dangers* With seedless raisins.
(*Paris,* f. 56v)

179. SWEET MILK (LAC DULCE)

Nature: In general, it has a nature o moderate warmth, leaning toward warm *Optimum:* That which comes from sheep *Usefulness:* For the chest and the lungs *Dangers:* For those suffering from fever and headaches. *Neutralization of th Dangers:* With seedless raisins. *Effects* It is good nourishment and is suitable fo moderate complexions, for adolescents, i Summer, and in Southerly regions.
(*Vienna,* f. 59)

80. SWEET MILK (LAC DULCE)

Nature: Of moderate warmth or sweetly warm. *Optimum:* That which comes from young sheep. *Usefulness:* For the chest and lungs. *Dangers:* For fevers. *Neutralization of the Dangers:* With seedless raisins.
(*Casanatense,* f. CXI)

81. LETTUCE (LACTUCE)

Nature: (According to Johannicus), cold and humid in the third degree. *Optimum:* The kind with large, lemon-colored leaves. *Usefulness:* It soothes insomnia and gonorrhea. *Dangers:* For coitus and for the eyesight. *Neutralization of the Dangers:* By mixing it with celery.
(*Paris,* f. 28)

182. LETTUCE (LACTUCE)

Nature: Cold and humid in the third degree. *Optimum:* The kind with large, lemon-colored leaves. *Usefulness:* It soothes insomnia and gonorrhea. *Dangers:* For coitus and for the eyesight. *Neutralization of the Dangers:* By mixing it with celery.
(*Casanatense,* f. LI)

183. SWEET MARJORAM (MAIORANA)

Nature: Warm and dry in the third degree. *Optimum:* The kind with a stronger aromatic power. It helps the stomach, the brain, all the intestines, and removes occlusions of the brain. *Dangers:* None, if it is not abused.
(*Paris,* f. 30)

184. SWEET MARJORAM (MAIORANA)

Nature: Warm and dry in the third degree. *Optimum:* The kind with a strong aromatic power. *Usefulness:* It is good for the stomach, the brain, all the intestines, and removes occlusions of the brain. *Dangers:* None. if it is not abused.
(*Casanatense,* CLX)

185. SOUR APPLES (MALLA ACCETOSA)

Nature: (According to Theodorus), cold and humid in the second degree. *Optimum:* . . . *Usefulness:* For fainting. *Dangers:* For the joints. *Neutralization of the Dangers:* With yellow-colored wine.
(*Paris,* f. 7)

188. THE FRUIT OF THE MANDRAGORA (FRUCTUS MANDRAGORAE)

Nature: Cold in the third degree, dry in the second. *Optimum:* The large and fragrant ones. *Usefulness:* When smelled, it soothes headaches; when spread on the skin, it acts against elephantiasis and black infections of the skin. *Dangers:* It dulls the senses and induces sleepiness. *Neutralization of the Dangers:* With the fruit of the ivy plant.
(*Casanatense,* f. LXXIII)

189. SORGHUM (MELITA)

Nature: Cold and dry in the first degree. *Optimum:* Reddish, well ripened, and large. *Usefulness:* For rough mountaineers who engage in heavy work. *Dangers:* It is slow and difficult to digest. *Neutralization of the Dangers:* With aromas and plenty of yeast. *Effects:* It generates melancholy humors and is more suitable for warm and rough temperaments, for young people, in Winter, in cold and mountainous regions.
(*Vienna,* f. 48v)

190. SORGHUM (MELEGA)

Nature: Cold and dry in the second degree. *Optimum:* The white kind. *Usefulness:* For peasants and the swine. *Dangers:* Causes swellings and melancholy. *Neutralization of the Dangers:* With foods that generate merriment.
(*Casanatense,* f. XC)

186. SOUR APPLES (MALA ACETOSA)

Nature: Cold in the second degree, humid in the first. *Optimum:* Those which are very juicy. *Usefulness:* For an inflamed liver. *Dangers:* For the chest and the voice. *Neutralization of the Dangers:* With foods mixed with honey.
(*Casanatense,* f. XI)

187. THE FRUIT OF THE MANDRAGORA (FRUCTUS MANDRAGORAE)

Nature: (According to Johannes), cold in the third degree and dry in the second. *Optimum:* The large and fragrant ones. *Usefulness:* When smelled, it soothes headaches; when spread on the skin, it acts against elephantiasis and black infections of the skin. *Dangers:* It dulls the senses and induces sleepiness. *Neutralization of the Dangers:* With the fruits of the ivy plant.
(*Paris,* f. 85)

1. SWEET MELONS (*MELONES ULCES*)

Nature: (According to Jesus), cold in ⁚ second degree and humid in the ⁚rd. *Optimum:* The kind called *smar-andi*. *Usefulness:* They cure gallstones ⁚ purify the skin. *Dangers:* They purge ⁚ stomach. *Neutralization of the Dan-⁚rs:* With good wine or sour syrup.
⁚ris, f. 37)

2. SWEET MELONS (*MELONES ULCES*)

⁚ture: Cold in the second degree and ⁚mid in the third. *Optimum:* The kind ⁚led *smaracandi*. *Usefulness:* They re-⁚ve gallstones and clean the skin. *Dan-⁚rs:* They purge the stomach. *Neutral-⁚tion of the Dangers:* With good wine ⁚ sour syrup.
⁚asanatense, f. XXXV)

193. PALESTINIAN MELONS (*MELONES PALESINII*)

Nature: (According to Albulcasem), cold and humid in the second degree. *Optimum:* Those which are sweet and watery. *Usefulness:* For acute illnesses. *Dangers:* For digestion. *Neutralization of the Dangers:* With barley sugar.
(Paris, f. 38)

194. INDIAN AND PALESTINIAN MELONS (*MELONES INDI ET PALESTINI*)

Indian-Palestinian melons are lemon-colored, large, and sweet watermelons. *Nature:* Cold and humid in the second degree; at other times in the third degree. *Optimum:* The large, sweet, and watery ones. *Usefulness:* For warm, acute illnesses. *Dangers:* They cause blockages to the digestion. *Neutralization of the Dangers:* With barley sugar or plain sugar. *Effects:* They generate watery blood and are suitable for warm temperaments, for young people, in Summer, and in the Southerly regions.
(Vienna, f. 22)

195. TASTELESS MELONS (*MELONES INSIPIDI*)

Nature: (According to Galen), cold and humid in the first degree. *Optimum:* Ripened ones. *Usefulness:* They stimulate urination. *Dangers:* They cause pain. *Neutralization of the Dangers:* By eating other foods after consuming them.
(Paris, f. 37v)

196. TASTELESS MELONS (*MELONES INSIPIDI*)

Nature: Cold and humid in the third degree. *Optimum:* Ripe ones. *Usefulness:* They stimulate urination. *Dangers:* They cause pain. *Neutralization of the Dangers:* By eating other foods after consuming them.
(Casanatense, f. XXXVI)

199. MUST *(MUSTUM)*

Nature: (According to Albulcasem), warm and humid in the second degree. *Optimum:* Clear must, just pressed. *Usefulness:* Fattens the body. *Dangers:* Causes flatulence. *Neutralization of the Dangers:* With pomegranate wine.
(Paris, f. 76)

200. TURNIPS *(NAPONES)*

Nature: Warm in the first degree, humid in the middle of the second degree. *Optimum:* The fresh, sweet, garden variety. *Usefulness:* They cause urination and sediments. *Dangers:* They cause flatulence and swellings. *Neutralization of the Dangers:* With pepper and aromas. *Effects:* They provide sufficiently good nourishment and are suitable for cold and dry temperaments, for people of all ages, in the Fall, and in the Northerly regions.
(Vienna, f. 51)

201. TURNIPS *(NAPONES)*

Nature: Warm in the second degree, humid in the first. *Optimum:* The kind that is long, wrinkled, and dark. *Usefulness:* They increase the sperm and make the flesh less susceptible to swellings. *Dangers:* They cause occlusions in the veins and in the pores. *Neutralization of the Dangers:* By stewing them twice and then cooking them with very fat meats.
(Casanatense, f. XCVII)

197. MILLET *(MILIUM)*

Nature: Cold in the first degree, dry in the second. *Optimum:* Fresh, white, and full. *Usefulness:* It is good for an inflamed stomach and for the flux of colic. It quenches thirst, especially when it is boiled in water. *Dangers:* For weak stomachs and intestines. *Neutralization of the Dangers:* Well cooked and consumed with sweet almond oil and sugar. *Effects:* It generates thick blood, not good, and is suitable for warm and humid temperaments, for young people, in Summer, and in Southerly regions.
(Vienna, f. 47v)

198. MILLET *(MILIUM)*

Nature: Cold in the first degree, dry in the second. *Optimum:* The kind that has been left in the field for longer than three months. *Usefulness:* For those who desire to refresh their stomachs and for the drying out of superfluous humors. *Dangers:* Not very nourishing. *Neutralization of the Dangers:* By consuming it with very nourishing substances.
(Casanatense, f. LXXXVIII)

2. SNOW AND ICE (NIX ET GLACIES)

Nature: Cold and humid in the third degree. *Optimum:* The kind formed from sweet and good water. *Usefulness:* Improves the digestion. *Dangers:* Causes coughing. *Neutralization of the Dangers:* drinking moderately first. *Effects:* Causes pain in the joints and paralysis. It is more suitable for warm temperaments, for young people, in Summer, and in Southerly regions.
(*Vienna,* f. 90)

3. SNOW AND ICE (NIX ET GLACIES)

Nature: Cold and humid in the second degree. *Optimum:* The kind formed from sweet and good water. *Usefulness:* Improves the digestion. *Dangers:* Causes coughing. *Neutralization of the Dangers:* By drinking moderately first.
(*Casanatense,* f. CLXXIV)

204. BARLEY (ORDIUM)

Nature: (According to Johannes), cold and dry in the first degree. *Optimum:* The kind that is not excessively large and white. *Usefulness:* It increases the expulsive capacity and is easily digested. *Dangers:* It causes slight pain. *Neutralization of the Dangers:* By toasting it.
(*Paris,* f. 47v)

205. BARLEY (ORDIUM)

Nature: Cold and dry in the second degree. *Optimum:* The white kind, large and fresh. *Usefulness:* Improves the faculty of expulsion and is easily digested. *Dangers:* It causes slight pain. *Neutralization of the Dangers:* Well toasted. *Effects:* It generates good humors and is suitable for warm temperaments, for young people, in Summer, and in warm regions.
(*Vienna,* f. 44)

206. GOOSE EGGS (OUA ANSERUM)

Nature: Of moderate warmth and large. *Optimum:* Those that are half-cooked. *Usefulness:* For those engaged in heavy work. *Dangers:* For colic, flatulence, and vertigo. *Neutralization of the Dangers:* With oregano and salt.
(*Paris,* f. 61)

207. GOOSE EGGS (OUA ANSERUM)

Nature: Of moderate warmth and large. *Optimum:* Those that are half-cooked. *Usefulness:* For those engaged in heavy work. *Dangers:* For colic, flatulence, and vertigo. *Neutralization of the Dangers:* With oregano and salt.
(*Casanatense,* f. CXXV)

208. CHICKEN EGGS (*OVA GALINARUM*)

Nature: The albumen is cold and humid, the yolk is warm and humid. *Optimum:* The fresh and large ones. *Usefulness:* They increase coitus and are very nourishing. *Dangers:* They slow down digestion and cause freckles. *Neutralization of the Dangers:* By consuming only the yolk.
(*Paris,* f. 60)

209. PANIC GRASS (*PANICUM*)

Nature: Cold and dry in the second degree. *Optimum:* Well ripened and large. *Usefulness:* For warm and humid bodies. *Dangers:* It aggravates . . . and has an astringent effect. *Neutralization of the Dangers:* With barley sugar.
(*Paris,* f. 53)

210. PANIC GRASS (*PANICHUM*)

Nature: Cold in the first degree, dry in the second. As for its best selection, usefulness, and disadvantages, see "Millet." (Vienna, f. 48)

211. UNLEAVENED BREAD (*PANIS AZIMUS*)

Nature: (According to Hippocrates), cold and dry in the second degree. *Optimum:* Heavily salted and well baked. *Usefulness:* For bodies that have an abundance of salt. *Dangers:* Causes swellings and flatulence. *Neutralization of the Dangers:* With old wine.
(*Paris,* f. 55)

212. MILLET BREAD (*PANIS MILIJ*)

Nature: Cold and dry in the second degree. *Optimum:* Thin and well baked. *Usefulness:* For sanguine bodies. *Dangers:* Overheats the stomach. *Neutralization of the Dangers:* Through leavening and perfect baking.
(*Paris,* f. 56)

213. VERY FINE WHITE BREAD (*PANIS DE SIMILA IDEST PANIS ALRASSIMUS*)

Nature: (According to Hippocrates), temperate in warmth in the second degree. *Optimum:* That which is well baked and lemon-colored. *Usefulness:* Fattens the body. *Dangers:* Causes occlusions. *Neutralization of the Dangers:* Through thorough leavening.
(*Paris,* f. 54)

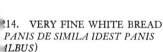

214. VERY FINE WHITE BREAD (PANIS DE SIMILA IDEST PANIS ALBUS)

Nature: Of moderate warmth in the second degree. *Optimum:* That which is well baked and lemon-colored. *Usefulness:* Fattens the body. *Dangers:* Causes occlusions in the viscera. *Neutralization of the Dangers:* Through thorough leavening.
(*Casanatense,* f. CXIX)

215. COOKED BREAD (PANIS SUB TESTO COCTUS)

Nature: (According to Johannes), moderately cold in the second degree. *Optimum:* That which is leavened and thin. *Usefulness:* For active bodies. *Dangers:* Burdens the stomach and produces gallstones. *Neutralization of the Dangers:* With . . . meats and broths.
(*Paris,* f. 55v)

216. PARTRIDGES (PERDICES)

Nature: (According to Johannes), of moderate warmth. *Optimum:* Those which are fat and juicy. *Usefulness:* For convalescents. *Dangers:* For those who habitually carry heavy loads. *Neutralization of the Dangers:* By preparing them with leavened dough.
(*Paris,* f. 67v)

217. PARTRIDGES (PERDICES)

Nature: Warm in the second degree and of moderate humidity. *Optimum:* Fat ones and juicy. *Usefulness:* For convalescing people. *Dangers:* For those who engage in heavy work and carry heavy loads. *Neutralization of the Dangers:* When cooked with leavened dough. *Effects:* They generate good blood and are more suitable for moderate temperaments, for children and old people, in Spring, and in the Northerly regions.
(*Vienna,* f. 67v)

218. PEACHES (PERSICA)

Nature: (According to Rufus), . . . in the second degree. *Optimum:* The kind called *muscati.* *Usefulness:* For hot fevers. *Dangers:* They corrupt humors. *Neutralization of the Dangers:* With fragrant wine.
(*Paris,* f. 3v)

219. PURSLANE (PORTULACA ET CITAREIA)

Nature: Cold in the third degree, humid in the first. *Optimum:* The kind with the largest and most tender leaves. *Usefulness:* Against toothache; it also removes warts. *Dangers:* For the sperm and coitus. *Neutralization of the Dangers:* With sylvan juices.
(*Rouen,* f. 26)

220. *SAVICH* OR BARLEY SOUP (*SAVICH IDEST PULTES TRITICI*)

Nature: Warm and dry in the second degree. *Optimum:* That which is toasted over moderate heat. *Usefulness:* For humid intestines. *Dangers:* Irritates the chest. *Neutralization of the Dangers:* By rinsing it with warm water.
(*Casanatense*, f. LXXXI)

221. RICOTTA (*RECOCTA*)

Nature: Cold and humid. *Optimum:* That which is made from pure milk. *Usefulness:* It nourishes and fattens. *Dangers:* It causes occlusions and is difficult to digest. *Neutralization of the Dangers:* With butter and honey. *Effects:* It generates thick blood and is more suitable to warm and vigorous temperaments, to young people, at the beginning of Summer, and in mountainous regions.
(*Vienna*, f. 62)

222. RICE (*RIZON*)

Nature: (According to Johannes), warm and dry in the second degree. *Optimum:* The kind called *margaritarum* which increases in size while cooking. *Usefulness:* For an inflamed stomach. *Dangers:* For people suffering from colic. *Neutralization of the Dangers:* With oil and milk.
(*Paris*, f. 48)

223. RICE BREAD (*PANIS RIZON*)

Nature: Cold and dry in the second degree. *Optimum:* That which is made from the rice called *margaritino*. *Usefulness:* Imparts a nice color to the face and fattens the body. *Dangers:* It is difficult to digest. *Neutralization of the Dangers:* With exercise and baths.
(*Rouen*, f. 35v)

224. SAGE (*SALUIA*)

Nature: Warm and humid in the second degree. *Optimum:* The domestic variety. *Usefulness:* For paralysis and the nerves. *Dangers:* Removes the dark color from the hair. *Neutralization of the Dangers:* In rinses that contain myrtle and the oriental crocus.
(*Paris*, f. 34)

225. SAGE (SALUIA)

Nature: Warm in the first degree, dry in the second. *Optimum:* The domestic variety from the garden; however, the wild variety is stronger when heated. *Usefulness:* It is good for the stomach and for cold illnesses of the nerves. *Dangers:* It is digested slowly. *Neutralization of the Dangers:* With an infusion of apples. *Effects:* It generates thick blood, sometimes warm, and is suitable for cold temperaments, for old people, in Winter, and in cold regions.
(*Vienna*, f. 37v)

226. RYE (SILIGO)

Nature: Cold and dry in the first degree. *Optimum:* Full and well ripened. *Usefulness:* It dilutes the sharpness of the humors. *Dangers:* For those suffering from colic or from melancholy. *Neutralization of the Dangers:* With plenty of wheat.
(*Paris*, f. 47)

227. RYE (SILIGO)

Nature: Cold and dry in the second degree. *Optimum:* Fresh, large, and full. *Usefulness:* It represses the sharpness of the humors. *Dangers:* It is difficult to digest. *Neutralization of the Dangers:* With plenty of wheat. *Effects:* It generates heavy humors that occlude and is more suitable for warm and strong temperaments who perform physical exercises; for young people, in Winter, in the Northerly and in mountainous regions.
(*Vienna*, f. 46v)

228. SPELT (SPELTA)

Nature: Of temperate quality. *Optimum:* The heavier kind. *Usefulness:* For the chest, the lungs, and coughing. *Dangers:* It is bad for the stomach and disturbs the mind. *Neutralization of the Dangers:* . . .
(*Paris*, f. 48v)

229. SPELT (SPELTA)

Nature: Moderately warm. *Optimum:* That which is heavy and well ripened. *Usefulness:* For the chest, the lungs, and coughing. *Dangers:* For weak stomachs, and it is less nourishing than wheat. *Neutralization of the Dangers:* By consuming it with anise. *Effects:* It generates good blood and is more suitable for temperate complexions, for all ages, in Winter, and in all regions.
(*Vienna*, f. 47)

230. THERIAC (*TIRIACA*)

Nature: Warm and cold. *Optimum:* The kind that frees. . . .
Usefulness: Against poisons and against warm and cold illnesses. *Dangers:* It causes insomnia. *Neutralization of the Dangers:* With cooling substances such as barley water.
(*Paris,* f. 87v)

231. THERIAC (*TRIACHA*)

Nature: Warm and dry. *Optimum:* . . .
Usefulness: Against poisons and warm swellings. *Dangers:* Causes insomnia. *Neutralization of the Dangers:* With cooling substances such as barley water.
(*Casanatense,* f. C)

232. WHEAT PASTA (*FORMENTINI*)

Nature: (According to Albulcasem), cold and humid in the second degree. *Optimum:* That which has been prepared with great care. *Usefulness:* For the chest and the throat. *Dangers:* For weak intestines. *Neutralization of the Dangers:* With barley sugar.
(*Paris,* f. 50)

233. WHEAT PASTA (*TRIJ*)

Nature: Warm and humid in the seco degree. *Optimum:* That which is p pared with great care. *Usefulness:* the chest and the throat. *Dangers:* weak intestines. *Neutralization of Dangers:* With barley sugar. [Accord to Avicenna, it is of a warm nature its humidity is superfluous. (Annotat by a second hand, of uncertain date.)]
(*Casanatense,* f. LXXXIV)

234. GRAPES (*UUE*)

Nature: (According to Johannes), wa in the first degree and humid in the s ond. *Optimum:* . . . watery, that sa guards one from poison. *Usefuln* Nourishes, purifies, and fattens. *Dang* Causes thirst. *Neutralization of the D* gers: With sour pomegranates.
(*Paris,* f. 2)

235. GRAPES *(UUE)*

Nature: Warm in the first degree, humid in the second. *Optimum:* The white kind, watery and with a thin skin. *Usefulness:* Cleans the intestines and accelerates the formation of fats. *Dangers:* Causes thirst. *Neutralization of the Dangers:* With sour pomegranates. *Effects:* It generates good blood and is primarily suitable for cold temperaments by nature, for very old people, in the Fall, and in the Northerly regions.
(Vienna, f. 5)

236. WESTERLY WIND *(VENTUS OCCIDENTALIS)*

Nature: Moderately dry in the second degree, at other times in the first. *Optimum:* Coming from the North. *Usefulness:* It improves the digestion. *Dangers:* It is bad for trembling and cold. *Neutralization of the Dangers:* With heat and heavy clothing. It is more suitable for temperate complexions, for all ages, in Spring, and in Eastern Regions.
(Vienna, f. 57v)

237. EASTERLY WIND *(VENTUS ORIENTALIS)*

Nature: Moderately warm in the second degree. *Optimum:* That which crosses meadows and rainy places. *Usefulness:* Raises the spirits. *Dangers:* Harms the eyes and the heart. *Neutralization of the Dangers:* With flower water. It is suitable for temperate complexions, for any age, in Spring, and in the Eastern regions.
(Vienna, f. 57)

238. NORTHERLY WIND *(VENTUS SEPTENTRIONALIS)*

Nature: Cold in the third degree, dry in the second. *Optimum:* The one that crosses over sweet waters. *Usefulness:* It sharpens the senses. *Dangers:* It is bad for the chest and for coughing. *Neutralization of the Dangers:* With baths and heavy clothing. It is suitable for warm and humid temperaments, for young people, and in Southerly regions.
(Vienna, f. 58v)

241. VIOLETS (VIOLE)

Nature: Cold in the first degree, humid in the second. *Optimum:* Lapis-lazuli colored, with many leaves. *Usefulness:* When smelled, they calm frenzies; when drunk, they purify bilious humors. *Dangers:* They are bad for catarrh caused by the cold. *Effects:* None. They are suitable for warm and dry temperaments, for young people, in Summer, and in the Southerly regions.
(*Vienna*, f. 39)

242. VOMIT (UOMITUS)

Nature: Emission of humors by the way contrary to that of foods. *Optimum:* The kind that is not difficult for those with ample chests. *Usefulness:* For the stomach and the inferior extremities of the body. *Dangers:* For the brain and for the chest of narrow dimensions. *Neutralization of the Dangers:* By blindfolding and by the use of an appropriate apparatus.
(*Paris*, f. 89)

243. VOMIT (UOMITUS)

Nature: Emission of humors extracted through the way of foods. *Optimum:* The kind that is not difficult for people with ample chests. *Usefulness:* For the stomach and for the inferior extremities of the body. *Dangers:* For the brain and for chests of narrow dimensions. *Neutralization of the Dangers:* By blindfolding and by the use of an appropriate apparatus.
(*Casanatense*, f. CXCII)

239. SPRING (VER)

Nature: Warm and moderately humid in the second degree. *Optimum:* Its middle period. *Usefulness:* It is universally good for all animals, and for the products that germinate from the earth. *Dangers:* It harms humid bodies because it causes corruption in them. *Neutralization of the Dangers:* By purifying the body. Good humors are generated during it. It is particularly suitable for the cold or dry or moderate temperaments, for young people and others, in temperate regions and in almost all the others.
(*Vienna*, f. 55v)

240. YELLOW-COLORED WINE (VINUM CITRINUM)

Nature: Warm and dry in the second degree. *Optimum:* The clear one of the year. *Usefulness:* Against poisons, especially cold ones. *Dangers:* Placates the desire for coitus. *Neutralization of the Dangers:* With sour quince. *Effects:* It generates acute bilious humors and is more suitable for cold temperaments, for very old people, in Winter, and in Northerly regions.
(*Vienna*, f. 87v)

TABLE OF CONCORDANCE

The subject is indicated as it appears in the Vienna codex, following Unterkircher's study. The titles in the other codices indicate those subjects that are not available in the Vienna codex. For the Rouen codex, the pages without illustration are marked with an asterisk.

	Vienna	Casanatense	Paris	Liège	Rouen
Medico in cattedra	4	I	1	1v	1
Absintium	37	LXVII	33v	15v	—
Acetum	85v	CLXIV	77v	58v	—
Adeps et pinguedo	81v	CLV	75	49	—
Aer epidinicus	—	—	101	36v	51*
Agrestum	85	CLXIII	75v	56	—
Alae et colla	—	—	—	—	36v
Alea	26	XLV	25	—	23
Ambra	84v	CLXII	—	—	—
Amidum	—	—	—	32	—
Amigdale amare	—	—	10	—	33
Amigdale dulces	18v	XXIX	10v	9v	32v
Amilum	43	LXXIX	49v	—	—
Anates et anseres	69v	CXXXII	71v	55	—
Aneti	32	LVII	40v	—	13
Anguille	—	—	—	61v	39*
Animalia castrata	71	CXXXIV	65	45	—
Anisum	41	LXXV	23v	22	—
Apium	30	LIII	28v	—	11
Aqua aliminoxa	90v	CLXXIII	98	—	—
Aqua calida	89	CLXXII	97	—	—
Aqua caliditatis nimie	—	—	—	—	43*
Aqua canphore	—	—	—	—	45*
Aqua delectabilis caliditatis	—	—	—	76	42*
Aqua excellentis frigiditatis	—	—	—	—	41v*
Aqua fontium	88v	CLXIX	94	74	—
Aqua frigida	—	—	—	—	42v*
Aqua ordei	45	LXXXIII	52	—	—
Aqua pluuialis	89v	CLXXI	93v	74v	—
Aqua rosacea	93	CLXXVII	—	—	—
Aqua salsa	88	CLXX	97v	76v	—
Armoniaca	9v	XII	7v	7	6v
Assum in aere	—	—	—	—	38v*
Assum super carbones	—	—	—	—	38*
Auicule et durdi	106v	CCVIII	72	55v	52*
Autumpnus	54v	CII	103v	81v	—
Avelane	17v	XXV	11v	—	31v
Avena	—	—	49	30v	—
Bacha lauri	18	XXVI	20	—	32
Balneum	—	—	—	75v	41*
Basilicum citratum	39v	LXXII	22v	10v	—
Blete	27v	XLVIII	27	—	24v
Brodium cicerum	—	—	46	27v	—
Brugna	6	V	4	3v	3
Butirum	61	CXV	58	39	—
Camamille	—	—	80v	63	—
Camere et aer ipsius	—	—	—	78	50v*
Camere estivales	97	CLXXXVII	99	77v	—
Camere hyemales	97v	CLXXXVIII	98v	77	—
Camphora	94	CLXXXII	—	—	—
Cana melle	92v	CLXXVIII	—	—	—
Candele	95v	CLXXXVI	—	—	—
Candi	—	—	81v	62v	—
Cantus	103	CCIII	85v	—	—
Capari	24v	XLII	39	21	21v

	Vienna	Casanatense	Paris	Liège	Rouen
Capita animalium	76v	CXLVI	73	—	—
Carnes arietum	72v	CXXXVIII	61v	42	—
Carnes caprarum et proprie edorum	73	CXXXIX	62	43	—
Carnes gazelarum (Carnes capreolorum silvestrium)	71v	CXXXVI	64	45v	—
Carnes leporine	72	CXXXVII	64v	46	—
Carnes leporinae et silvestrium	—	—	91v	—	—
Carnes porcine	74v	CXLI	63v	44v	—
Carnes salite sicce	75	CXLIII	66	48	—
Carnes sufryxe	75v	CXLIV	—	—	—
Carnes sufrixe recentes	—	—	—	47	—
Carnes sufrixe salite	—	—	—	47v	—
Carnes uachine et camelorum	74	CXLII	63	44	—
Carnes vitulorum	73v	CXL	62v	43v	—
Carube	14v	XIX	13v	—	28v
Caseus recens	60	CXIII	58v	39v	—
Caseus vetus	60v	CXIV	59v	40 e 41	—
Casia fulnis	—	—	—	86	—
Castanee	17	XXIV	11	—	31
Caules	—	—	27v	—	44v*
Caules idest verze	—	—	29	—	—
Caules onati	23	XXXIX	—	20	—
Cefalones id est datili	12v	XXXI	16	—	25v
Cepe	25v	XLIV	24v	—	22v
Cerebra animalium	77	CXLVII	—	—	—
Cerosa acetosa	12	XVII	9v	8v	25
Cerosa dulcia	11v	XVI	9	9	8v
Cetrona	20	XXVII	18v	—	34v
Cicera	49	XCI	43v	24v	—
Citonia	8	IX	6	5v	5
Citra	19	XXX	15v e 18	82v	34
Cohitus	—	CXCVI	100v	69v	—
Coliandorum	—	—	—	13v	—
Confabulationes in sompnis	101	CXCV	90v	68v	—
Confabulator	100v	CXCIII	90	68	—
Corda animalium	78v	CL	—	—	—
Coria seu cutes	—	—	—	—	39v*
Coriandrum	—	—	31v	—	—
Conturnices	—	—	72v	—	37v*
Crochus	40v	LXXIV	—	—	—
Cucumeres et citruli	23v	XL	38v	20v	20v
Cucurbite	22v	XXXVIII	36v	18v	19v
Ebrietas	99	CXCI	88v	66v	—
Enula	35v	LXIV	35	17v	16v
Epata animalium	80	CLIII	73v	50	—
Equitatio	102	CXCVIII	93	71v	—
Eruca et Nasturtium (Rucola)	30v	LIV	21v	10	11v
Estas	54	CI	—	81	—
Exercitium lene	—	—	—	71	50*
Exercitium moderatum cum pila	—	—	—	—	49v*
Faba	49v	XCII	44	25	—
Faxani	68v	CXXX	67	52v	—
Faxioli	50v	XCIV	44v	26	—
Feniculus	41v	LXXVI	41	22v	—
Festuce	—	—	19	—	—
Fichus	4v	II	1v	—	1v
Ficus sice	56v	CV	2v	—	—
Foca ordeaceum, idest al certusia	—	—	—	—	48v*
Fructus mandragore	40	LXXIII	85	16v	—
Frumentum	42v	LXXVIII	46v	28	—

	Vienna	Casanatense	Paris	Liège	Rouen
Frumentum elixum	53	XCIX	51	33v	—
Funghi	—	—	—	85v	—
Galenga	32v	LVIII	40	—	13v
Galli	65	CXXIII	68v	54	—
Galline	—	—	69	50v	36*
Gambari	83	CLX	80	61	—
Gaudia	104v	CCIV	—	65	—
Geletina	76	CXLV	65v	46v	—
Glandes	15	XX	—	—	29
Granata acetosa	7v	VIII	5v	5	4v
Granata dulcia	7	VII	5	4v	4
Grues	70v	CXXXIII	70v	52	—
Herba piretri	29v	LII	21	—	10v
Hyemps	55	CIII	102	82	—
Intestina, id est busecha	81	CLVI	74v	48v	—
Ira	98v	CXC	88	66	—
Juiube	15v	XXI	13	—	29v
Jumpenis	—	—	—	85	—
Lac acetosum	59v	CXII	57	38	—
Lac coagulatum (Juncata)	61v	CXVI	57v	38v	—
Lac dulce	59	CXI	56v	37v	—
Lactuce	29	LI	28	—	10
Lamprete	84	CLXI	79v	60v	—
Langune	—	—	—	19v	—
Lentes	—	—	45	26v	—
Lilia	38v	LXX	84	12	—
Liquiritia	42	LXXVII	41v	18	—
Lisergia	—	—	—	25v	—
Liuistichum	36	LXV	32v	14v	—
Luctatio	96v	CLXXXV	95v	72	—
Lupini	51v	XCVIII	45v	27	—
Maiorana	33v	LX	30	—	14v
Mala acetosa	9	XI	7	6v	6
Mala dulcia	8v	X	6v	6	5v
Marubium	36v	LXVI	33	15	—
Mel	94v	CLXXXI	82	63v	—
Melita (Melega)	48v	XC	53v	—	—
Melones dulces	21	XXXV	37	20	18
Melones indi et palestini	22	XXXVII	38	—	19
Melones insipidi	21v	XXXVI	37v	19	18v
Melongiana	31v	XLI	25v	—	21
Menta	34	LXI	30v	—	15
Mesch, id est Cicerchia	50	XCIII	36	—	—
Milium	47v	LXXXVIII	52v	31	—
Mirtus	—	—	20v	—	—
Mora acerba	—	—	19v	—	—
Motus	102v	CCII	92	70	—
Muscus	93v	CLXXX	—	—	—
Musse	20v	XXXIV	17	—	17v
Mustum	—	—	76	56v	—
Nabach id est Cedrum	11	XV	—	—	8
Napones	51	XCVII	43	24	—
Nespula	10v	XIV	8v	8	7v
Nix et glacies	90	CLXXIV	96v	75	—
Nuces	16	XXII	12	—	30
Nux indie	14	XVIII	12v	—	28
Oculi animalium	77v	CXLVIII	—	—	—
Oleum amigdalarum	91	CLXXV	—	—	—
Oleum olive	91v	CLXXVI	15	—	—
Oleum violaceum	—	—	—	—	43v*
Olive nigre	16v	XXIII	14v	—	30v

	Vienna	Casanatense	Paris	Liège	Rouen
Ordium	44	LXXXI	47v	29	—
Organare cantum uel sonare	103v	CC	86	—	—
Ova anserum	66	CXXV	61	—	—
Ova austrum	—	—	—	42	—
Ova galinacea	65v	CXXIV	60	41v	—
Ova perdicum	66v	CXXVI	60v	—	—
Ozimum citratum (Basilicum gariofolatum)	31	LV	22 e 84v	11	—
Panicum	48	LXXXIX	53	31v	—
Panis azimus	64	CXXI	55	35v	—
Panis de fumo vel faculis	—	—	—	—	35*
Panis de simila	63	CXIX	54	34v	—
Panis milii	64v	CXXII	56	36	—
Panis opus	63v	CXX	54v	35	—
Panis rizon	—	—	—	—	35v
Panis sub testo coctus	—	—	55v	—	—
Passule	56	CV	3	—	—
Pastinace	28	XLIX	34v	17	9
Pavones	70	CXXXV	71	54v	—
Pedes et tibie	78	CXLIX	—	—	—
Perdices	67v	CXXVIII	67v	53	—
Persica	5v	IV	3v	—	2v
Petrosillum	34v	LXII	31	13	15v
Pines	19v	XXVIII	14	—	17
Pira	6v	VI	4v	4	3v
Pisca	—	—	—	3	—
Pisces infusi in aceto	83v	CLIX	78v	59v	—
Pisces recentes	82	CLVII	78	59	—
Pisces saliti	82v	CLVIII	79	60	—
Pori	25	XLIII	24	—	22
Portulaca et citareia	—	—	—	—	26
Puli columbini	67	CXXVII	69v	51	—
Pultes ordei	44v	LXXXII	51v	34	—
Pultes tritici	43v	LXXX	50v	33	—
Purgatio	—	—	—	—	51v*
Qualee	68	CXXIX	68	53v	—
Quies	—	CXCVII	92v	70v	—
Rafani	52	XCV	42	23	—
Rape	52v	XCVI	42v	23v	—
Recocta	62	CXVII	59	40v	—
Regio meridionalis	—	—	—	83	53v*
Regio occidentalis	—	—	87	84	53*
Regio orientalis	—	—	—	83v	52v*
Regio septentrionalis	—	—	—	82	—
Ribes	—	—	—	—	33v
Rizon	46	LXXXV	48	29v	—
Rob de ribes	—	—	—	—	48*
Roxe	38	LXIX	83	64	—
Rusuri id est datili	13	XXXII	16v	—	27
Ruta	35	LXIII	32	14	16
Rutab id est datilus	13v	XXXIII	17v	—	27v
Sal	62v	CXVIII	66v	—	—
Salvia	37v	LXVIII	34	16	—
Scariola	—	—	35v	—	26v
Sicomuri	10	XIII	8	7v	7
Siligo	46v	LXXXVI	47 e 102v	28v	—
Sinapi	24	LVI	23	11v	12v
Siropus acetosus	95	CLXXXIII	—	—	45v*
Siropus de citoniis	—	—	—	—	46*
Siropus de papaveribus	—	—	—	—	46v*
Siropus rosatius	—	—	—	—	47*

	Vienna	Casanatense	Paris	Liège	Rouen
Siropus talep, confectus in aqua rosata	—	—	—	—	47v*
Sompnus	100	CXCIV	89v	—	—
Sonare et balare	104	CCI	—	64v	—
Spargus	26v	XLVI	26	—	23v
Spelta	47	LXXXVII	48v	30	—
Sperma	—	—	—	—	49*
Spinachie	27	XLVII	26v	—	24
Splenes	80v	CLIV	74	49v	—
Tartufule	28v	L	39v	21v	9v
Testiculi	79v	CLII	—	—	—
Triacha	53v	C	87v	37	—
Trifolium	—	—	—	—	84v
Trii	45v	LXXXIV	50	32v	—
Turtures	69	CXXXI	70	51v	—
Ubera animalium	79	CLI	—	—	—
Uve	5	III	2	2v	2
Venatio terrestris	96	CLXXXIV	—	72v	—
Ventus meridionalis	58	CVII	101v	78v	—
Ventus occidentalis	57v	CX	100	79v	—
Ventus orientalis	57	CIX	99v	80	—
Ventus septentrionalis	58v	CVIII	—	79	—
Ver	55v	CIV	103	80v	—
Verecondia	98	CLXXXIX	86v	65v	—
Vestis lanea	105	CCVI	96	73v	—
Vestis linea	105v	CCVII	94v	73	—
Vestis de seta	106	CCV	95	—	—
Vigilie	101v	CXCIX	91	69	—
Vinum	—	—	—	57	—
Vinum album	86	CLXV	—	—	—
Vinum citrinum	87v	CLXVIII	76v	58	—
Vinum de dactilis	—	—	—	—	40v*
Vinum incipiens fieri acetosum	—	—	—	—	40*
Vinum rubeum grossum	87	CLXVII	77	—	—
Vinum vetus odoriferum	86v	CLXVI	—	57v	—
Viole	39	LXXI	83v	12v	—
Vomitus	99v	CXCII	89	67	—
Ysopus	33	LIX	29v	—	14
Xilo aloes	—	—	—	—	44*
Zucharum	92	CLXXIX	81	62	—

BIBLIOGRAPHY

1760

Casiri, *Bibliotheça arabico-ispana Escurialensis*, I, II, Madrid.

1792

S. Assemani, *Catalogo dei codici manoscritti orientali della Bibliografia Naniana*, Padova.

1839

Catalogues des Livres composants la Bibliothèque de M.C. Leber, I, p. 65, Rouen.

1868

L. Delisle, *Le cabinet des Manuscrits de la Bibliothèque imperiale-nationale*, Parigi, t. I; 1874 t. II; 1881 t. III.

1875

M. Grandjean, *Bibliothèque de l'Université de Liège*, Catalogue des manuscrits, Liegi.

1875-79

F. D'Adda, *Indagini storiche artistiche e bibliografiche sulla libreria Visconteo-Sforzesca del castello di Pavia*, Milano.

1885

F. D'Adda - Mongeri, *L'arte del minio nel ducato di Milano dal sec. XIII al XVI*, in « Archivio Storico Lombardo », XII, pp. 330-356; 528-557; 759-796.

1886

G. Camus, *L'opera salernitana 'Circa instans' ed il testo primitivo del Grand Herbier*, in « Memorie dell'Accad. delle Scienze di Modena », II, IV.

G. Mazzatinti, *Inventario dei manoscritti italiani della Biblioteca Nazionale di Parigi*, Roma-Firenze.

1888

H. Omont, *Catalogue Général des manuscrits des Bibliothèques Publiques de France*, Departements, II, pp. 78-9.

1892

E. Dognée, *Un manuscrit inedit d'origine cordouane*, in « Boletín de la Real Academia de la historia », Madrid, XXI, pp. 399-461.

1895

J. von Schlosser, *Ein veronesisches Bilderbuch und die höfische Kunst des XVI. Jahrhunderts*, in « Jahrbuch der kunsthistorischen Sammlungen der allerhöchsten Kaiserhauses », Vienna, XVI (traduzione italiana e prefazione di Gian Lorenzo Mellini, 1965).

1896

L. Delisle, *Tacuinum sanitatis in medicina*, (Recensione a Schlosser, 1895), in « Journal des Savants », pp. 518-540.

1898

C. Brockelmann, *Geschichte der Arabischen Letteratur*, Weimar.

1901

P. Giacosa, *Magistri Salernitani nondum editi*, Roma.

1901-02

Lazzarini, *I libri di F. Carrara*, in « Atti e memorie della R. Acc. di Padova », XVIII, p. 29

1905

G. Fogolari, *Il ciclo dei mesi nella torre dell'Aquila a Trento*, in « Tridentum », VIII, pp. 174-85.

P. Toesca, *Michelino da Besozzo e Giovannino de' Grassi. Ricerche sull'antica pittura lombarda*, in « L'Arte », pp. 321-339.

1906

P. Toesca, *A proposito di Giovannino de' Grassi*, in « L'Arte », pp. 56-57.

1907

P. Toesca, *Di alcuni miniatori lombardi della fine del Trecento*, in « L'Arte », pp. 184-196.

1908

A. Muñoz, *Un Theatrum Sanitatis con miniature veronesi del secolo XIV nella Biblioteca Casanatense*, in « Madonna Verona », pp. 1-24.

1911

B. Kurth, *Ein Freskenzyklus im Adlerturm zu Trient*, in « Jahrbuch des Kunsthistorischen Institutes der k.k. Zentralkommission für Denkmalpflege », Vienna.

1912

P. Toesca, *La pittura e la miniatura nella Lombardia dai più antichi monumenti alla metà del Quattrocento*, Milano (II ediz. a cura di E. Castelnuovo con importante nota introduttiva e aggiornamento bibliografico, 1966).

1913

P. Toesca, *Ancora della pittura e miniatura in Lombardia*, in « L'Arte ».

1918

G. Carbonelli - Ravasini, *Commenti sopra alcune miniature e pitture italiane a soggetto medico*, Roma.

1919-25

E. De Toni, *Il Libro dei Semplici di Benedetto Rinio*, in « Memorie della Pont. Acc. delle Scienze », V, pp. 171-276; VII, pp. 275-398; VIII, pp. 123-264.

1921

C. Weigelt, *Giovannino de' Grassi*, in Thieme-Becker, *Künstler-Lexikon*, vol. XIV, Lipsia, pp. 534 sgg.

1925

P. D'Ancona, *La miniature italienne du Xe au XVIe siècles*, Parigi-Bruxelles.

1927

Singer, *The Herbal in Antiquity and its transmission to later Ages*, in « Journal of Hellenic Studies », XLVII, Londra.

1934

A. Morassi, *Storia della pittura nella Venezia Tridentina*, Roma.

1936-37

L. Messedaglia, *Le piante alimentari del Tacuinum Sanitatis, ms. miniato della Bibl. Naz. di Parigi*, in « Atti del R. Ist. Veneto di Scienze, Lett. ed Arti », XCVI, pp. 571-681.

1937

E. Berti Toesca, *Un erborario del Trecento*, in « La Bibliofila », pp. 341-53.

E. Berti Toesca, *Il Tacuinum Sanitatis della Biblioteca Nazionale di Parigi*, Bergamo.

C. Brockelmann, *Geschichte der arabischen Litteratur*, Leida (integrazione del vol. del 1898).

E. Trenkler, *Les principaux manuscrits a peintures de la Bibliothèque Nationale de Vienne, Manuscrits Italiens*, in « Bulletin de la Société Française de Reproductions de manuscrits a peintures », Parigi.

1938

Van Schendel, *Le dessin en Lombardie*, Bruxelles.

1939

G.L. Micheli, *L'enluminure du haut moyen âge et les influences irlandaises*, Bruxelles.

1939-40

Bibliothèque Nationale, Catalogue général des manuscrits latins, T. I, II, pubblicati sotto la direzione di Ph. Lauer (n. 1-2692), Parigi.

1940

L. Serra - S. Baglioni, *Theatrum Sanitatis codice 4182 della R. Bibl. Casanatense*, Roma.

1943

V. Leroquais, *Supplement aux livres d'heures manuscrits de la Bibliothèque Nationale*, Maçon.

1944

C. Baroni, *La scultura gotica lombarda*, Milano (recensione di E. Arslan, in « Archivio Storico Lombardo »).

1947

L. Coletti, *I Primitivi*, vol. III, *I Padani*, Novara.

M.L. Kaschitz, *Theatrum sanitatis*, Baden-Baden.

1948

O. Pächt, *Italian Illuminated Manuscripts*, mostra alla Bodleian Library di Oxford.

1948-49

Kunstschätze der Lombardei, mostra a Zurigo, catalogo per la parte manoscritti a cura di Paolo D'Ancona con la collaborazione di Teresa Rogledi Manni e Stella Matalon.

1949

E. Aeschlimann - P. D'Ancona, *Dictionnaire des miniaturistes*, 2ª ed., Milano.

R. Schlling, *Zürich, Kunstschätze der Lombardei, Die Miniaturmalerei*, in « Phoebus », pp. 186 sgg.

1950

A. Chastel - R. Longhi, *Recensione alla mostra parigina*, in « Paragone », n. 11, pp. 61 e sgg.

T. Gasparrini Leporace, *Un inedito erbario farmaceutico del Trecento*, in « Rivista delle scienze mediche e naturali ».

A. Marabottini, *Giovanni da Milano*, Firenze.

P. Pächt, *Early Italian Nature Studies*, in « Journal of the Warburg and Courtauld Institutes », pp. 13 sgg.

Trésors des Bibliothèques d'Italie, a cura di M. Salmi, L. de Felice Olivieri Sangiacomo, C. Arcamone Barletta, G. Muzzioli, L. Frattarolo, Parigi, Mostra alla Bibliothèque Nationale.

E. Wickersheimer, *Les Tacuina Sanitatis et leur traduction allemande par Michel Herr*, in « Bibl. d'Umanisme et Renaissance », XII, 1950, p. 84 e sgg.

1951

L. Messedaglia, *Veronesi e non lombardi i miniatori del Tacuinum Sanitatis*, in « Ist. Veneto di Scienze, Lett. ed Arti », CIX, II, pp. 95-112.

C. Nissen, *Die Botanische Buchillustration*, Stoccarda.

P. Toesca, *Il Trecento*, Torino.

P. Toesca, *L'Uffiziolo visconteo della collezione Landau-Finaly donato alla città di Firenze*, Firenze.

1952

Abenländische Buchmalerei, Catalogo della Mostra, Vienna.

C. Baroni - S. Samek Ludovici, *La pittura lombarda del Quattrocento*, Messina-Firenze.

C. Baroni - G.A. Dell'Acqua, *Tesori d'arte in Lombardia*, Milano.

Bibliothèque Nationale, Catalogue général des manuscrits latins (n. 2693-3012), sotto la direzione di J. Porcher.

Farès Bishr, *Un Herbier arabe illustré du XIV siècle*, in « Archeologica orientalia in memoriam Ernst Herzfeld », New York (recensione di S. Rice in « Ars orientalis », Michigan, I, 1954, p. 218).

N. Rasmo, *Nota sui rapporti tra Verona e l'Alto Adige nella pittura del tardo Trecento*, in « Cultura Atesina ».

S. Samek Ludovici, *L'alfabeto di Giovannino de' Grassi*, in « Linea grafica », pp. 117 sgg.

1952-53

O. Pächt, *Eine wiedergefundene Tacuinum Sanitatis Handschrift*, in « Münchner Jahrbuch der bildenden Kunst », pp. 172-80.

1953

E. Panofsky, *Meaning in the Visual Arts. Papers in and on Art History*, (traduz. italiana *Il significato delle arti visive*, Torino, 1962).

1953-54

Mostra storica nazionale della miniatura, Roma, 1953, a cura di G. Muzzioli, con introduzione di M. Salmi, Firenze, (II ediz. 1954).

1954

Die Entwicklung der zoologischen und botanischen Illustration von der Antike zur Renaissance, in « Kunst-Chronik, VII, pp. 138-9.

1955

C. Baroni, *La scultura del primo Quattrocento*, in « Storia di Milano », VI, Milano.

L. Messedaglia, *A proposito dei miniatori del Tacuinum Sanitatis*, in « Atti dell'Acc. di agricoltura, scienze e lettere di Verona », p. 541 e sgg.

E. Pellegrin, *La Bibliothèque des Visconti et des Sforza Ducs de Milan au XV siècle*, Parigi.

J. Porcher, *Manuscrits à peintures du XIII au XVI siècle*, Mostra a Parigi, Bibliothèque Nationale.

M. Salmi, *La miniatura italiana*, Milano.

M. Salmi, *La pittura e la miniatura gotica in Lombardia*, in « Storia di Milano », IV, pp. 544-564; V, pp. 815-874; VI, pp. 767-855.

1956

M. Salmi, *La Miniatura Italiana*, Milano, II edizione.

1958

Arte lombarda dai Visconti agli Sforza, Milano, introduzione di R. Longhi, le schede di R. Cipriani, F. Russoli, F. Mazzini, B. Belloni e M.L. Ferrari.

Da Altichiero a Pisanello, Mostra a Verona, Catalogo di L. Magagnato, prefazione di G. Fiocco.

C. Nissen, *Herbals of five centuries*, Zurigo.

C. Santoro, *I Codici miniati della Trivulziana*, Milano.

1959

Arte lombarda dai Visconti agli Sforza, a cura di G.A. Dell'Acqua, F. Russoli, R. Cipriani.

E. Pellegrin, *Notes sur divers manuscrits latins des Bibliothèque de Milan*, in « Bulletin d'Information de l'Institut de Recherche et d'Histoire des Textes », n. 7, pp. 9-10.

J. Porcher, *L'enluminure française*, Parigi.

1961

Edizione in facsimile del Taccuino di disegni di G. de' Grassi della Biblioteca di Bergamo, « Monumenta Bergomensia V », Bergamo.

1962

Europäische Kunst um 1400, Catalogo della Mostra, Vienna.

M.L. Gengaro, *Tra i più antichi codici latini della Biblioteca Ambrosiana*, in « Arte Lombarda ».

L. Magagnato, *Arte e civiltà del Medio Evo Veronese*, Verona.

1963

E. Arslan, *Riflessioni sulla pittura gotica « internazionale » in Lombardia nel tardo Trecento*, in « Arte lombarda », II, pp. 25 sgg.

O. Mazal e F. Unterkircher, *Katalog der abendländischen Handschriften der Oesterreichischen Nationalbibliothek*, *Series Nova*, Vienna.

1964

E. Arslan, *Aspetti della pittura lombarda nella seconda metà del Trecento*, in «Critica d'Arte », 1964, n. 61, pp. 33 sgg.; n. 64, pp. 44 sgg.

R. Pallucchini, *La pittura veneziana del Trecento*, Venezia-Roma.

A.M. Romanini, *L'architettura gotica in Lombardia*, Milano.

1965

Ambraser Kunst-und Wunderkammer, Catalogo della Mostra, Vienna.

G.L. Mellini, *Altichiero e Jacopo Avanzi*, Milano.

1966

E. Pirani, *La miniatura gotica*, Milano.

E. Wickersheimer, *Les manuscrits latins de medecine du haut moyen âge dans les bibliothèques de France*, Parigi (Ediz. C.N.R.S.).

1967

Facsimile del ms. series nova 2466 *Tacuinum sanitatis in medicina* della Biblioteca Nazionale di Vienna con commento, trascrizione e traduzione in tedesco di F. Unterkircher e traduzione in inglese di H. Saxer e C.H. Talbot.

Hamarneh Sami, *Index of Arabic Manuscripts on Medicine and Pharmacy at the National Library of Cairo* (testo inglese e arabo).

Huisman, *Les manuscrits arabes dans le monde*, Leida.

M. Meiss, *French Painting in the time of Jean de Berry*, Edimburgo.

A. Peroni, *Il San Michele di Pavia*, Milano [a cura della Cassa di Risparmio delle Provincie Lombarde].

F. Unterkircher, *European Illuminated Manuscripts in the Austrian National Library*, Londra.

1968

A. Griseri, *Jaquerio e il realismo gotico in Piemonte*, Torino.

1970

A. Cadei, *Giovannino de' Grassi nel taccuino di Bergamo*, in « Critica d'Arte ».

L. Cogliati Arano, *Due libri d'ore lombardi eseguiti verso il 1380*, in « Arte Lombarda », I.

L. Cogliati Arano, *Miniature Lombarde, codici miniati dall'VIII al XIV secolo*, introduzione di M.L. Gengaro, Milano [a cura della Cassa di Risparmio delle Provincie Lombarde].

« *Theatrum Sanitatis* » *di Ububchasym de Baldach*, Cod. 4182 della Bibl. Casanatense di Roma, a cura di A. Pazzini, E. Pirani, M. Salmi, trascrizione latina a cura di S. Samek Ludovici, Parma.

1971-72

L. García Ballester, *Los Mss. cientificos bajomedievales de la Biblioteca Universitaria de Granada*, in « Boletín de la Universidad de Granada », pp. 123-136.

1972

L. Cogliati Arano, *La scultura*, in *Il Duomo di Como*, Milano [a cura della Cassa di Risparmio delle Provincie Lombarde].

L. Donati, *Bibliografia della miniatura*, Firenze.

M. Meiss - E.W. Kirsch, *Les Heures de Visconti*, Parigi.

G. Paccagnini, *Pisanello e il ciclo cavalleresco di Mantova*, Milano, [1972].

N. Rasmo, *Affreschi medioevali atesini*, Milano, [1972].

1973

Trésors d'orient, Mostra alla Bibliotèque Nationale di Parigi.

LIST OF RELATED MANUSCRIPTS

Alessandria d'Egitto, Biblioteca Civica: ms. 3355 sez. araba

Ashburnham Place, appendix 101

Bergamo, Biblioteca Civica: Taccuino di disegni

Bevagna, ms. 9

Caen, ms. 92

Chantilly, Museo Condé: Très Riches Heures de Jan de Berry

Erfurt, ms. q. 228

Firenze, Biblioteca Laurenziana: ms. 18 sin. 7

Firenze, Biblioteca Nazionale: Offiziolo Visconti

Firenze, Biblioteca Nazionale: ms. Pal. 586

Granada, Biblioteca Universitaria: ms. C 67

Liegi, Biblioteca Universitaria: Tacuinum sanitatis, ms. 1041

Lipsia, ms. 1127

Londra, British Museum: Egerton ms. 747

Londra, British Museum: ms. Add. 3676

Lucca, Biblioteca: ms. 296

Milano, Biblioteca Ambrosiana: ms. B 41 Inf.

Milano, Biblioteca Ambrosiana: cod. D 84 Inf.

Milano, Biblioteca Ambrosiana: ms. R 70 Sup.

Milano, Biblioteca Trivulziana: Beroldo

Monaco, Biblioteca Nazionale: Offiziolo di Giovanni di Benedetto da Como

Parigi, Biblioteca Nazionale: De viris illustribus, ms. lat. 6069

Parigi, Biblioteca Nazionale: Frontino

Parigi, Biblioteca Nazionale: Guiron le Courtois

Parigi, Biblioteca Nazionale: Manfredus de Monte Imperiali

Parigi, Biblioteca Nazionale: Lancelot du lac

Parigi, Biblioteca Nazionale: ms. Smith Lesouëff 22

Parigi, Biblioteca Nazionale: Tacuinum sanitatis; ms. Lat. Nouv. Acq. 1673

Parigi, Biblioteca Nazionale: ms. Lat. 757

Parigi, Biblioteca Nazionale: ms. arabe 4947

Parigi, Biblioteca Nazionale: ms. 6977

Parigi, Biblioteca Nazionale: ms. 6977 A

Parigi, Biblioteca Nazionale: ms. Lat. 9333

Parigi, Biblioteca Nazionale: ms. 10264

Parigi, Biblioteca Nazionale: ms. 15362

Parigi, Ecole des Beaux-Arts: Trattato di Storia Naturale

Pisa, Seminario Arcivescovile di S. Caterina: ms. 7

Praga, Biblioteca del Museo Nazionale: Liber Viaticus di Johannes Noviforensis

Roma, Biblioteca Angelica: ms. 1082

Roma, Biblioteca Angelica: ms. 1501

Roma, Biblioteca Casanatense: Historia Plantarum, cod. lat. 459

Roma, Biblioteca Casanatense: Theatrum Sanitatis, ms. 4182

Roma, Biblioteca Vaticana: ms. 2426

Roma, Biblioteca Vaticana: ms. 2427

Rouen, Biblioteca Municipale: Tacuinum Sanitatis, ms. Leber 1088

Torino, Biblioteca Nazionale: ms. K. IV 3

Torino, Biblioteca Reale: mss. vari 129

Torino, Biblioteca Universitaria: cod. F. II 20

Venezia, Biblioteca Marciana: ms. lat. 315

Vienna, Biblioteca Nazionale: Dioscoride

Vienna, Biblioteca Nazionale: Evangeliario di Giovanni di Troppau - cod. 1182

Vienna, Biblioteca Nazionale: Tacuinum sanitatis, Ms. Series Nova 2644

Vienna, Biblioteca Nazionale: ms. 958

Vienna, Biblioteca Nazionale: ms. 2322

Vienna, Biblioteca Nazionale: ms. 2396

Vienna, Biblioteca Nazionale: ms. 5264